BENGALI COOKING

CHITRITA BANERJI, who was born and brought up in Calcutta, lived in Bangladesh for seven years before moving to the United States, where she now lives. After studying at Harvard University, she worked in journalism and broadcasting in Calcutta, London and Cambridge, Massachusetts. She has contributed to *Granta, Boston Magazine, The Phoenix* and a variety of other publications, and also translated both novels and short stories by modern Bengali authors.

BENGALI COOKING

Seasons and Festivals

Chitrita Banerji

Foreword by Deborah Madison

Decorations by Jane Smith

Serif

London

This edition first published 1997 by
Serif
47 Strahan Road
London E3 5DA

and

1436 Randolph Street
Chicago IL 60607

Originally published, in a slightly different form, as *Life and Food
in Bengal* by
Weidenfeld and Nicolson in 1991

British Library Cataloguing-in-Publication Data.
A catalogue record for this book is available from
the British Library.

Library of Congress Cataloging in Publication Data.
A catalog record for this book is available from
the Library of Congress.

ISBN 1 897959 29 X

Designed by Ralph Barnby.
Photoset in North Wales by
Derek Doyle & Associates, Mold, Flintshire.
Printed and bound in Great Britain by
Biddles of Guildford and King's Lynn.

CONTENTS

For my mother,
the inspired provider,
and in memory of
my father,
the discerning gourmet,
A Daughter's Gift

FOREWORD

The citizen of even a modestly-sized American city can decide each night whether to yield to the desire for Northern Italian food or give in to a yen for Sechuan, generic Chinese, Mexican, Vietnamese, or some other exotic cuisine. In New York, one needn't even leave home to enjoy a Turkish meal or a dinner of another cultural persuasion delivered in cartons. We don't blink an eye at such an array of culinary possibilities, nor do we necessarily look deeply into them. Diversity reigns in restaurants and in cookbooks, and there is a new urge for authenticity.

Books are now written to guide us not only through the familiar parts of foreign cuisines, but through the unknown territories as well, adopting recipes as needed so that we can provide ourselves with all kinds of things to eat that we never learned from our mothers. Of late, more care has been given by authors to get it right, to be authentic, and at least to go to the source if one doesn't come from the source. Today even the fledgling foodie knows that it's not quite right to say he or she likes Italian food. After all, what does food from the Veneto have to do with that from Sicily? We have at least come to recognise that there is no such thing as Italian food – or Mexican, French, Chinese, or Indian food for that matter – for food is more specific than that.

As we scrutinize cuisines ever more closely and try to skew them to the cultures from which they spring, we are attempting to connect food to life itself. Seldom has a book presented such a full-blown and lush awareness of the complex relationships between food and culture as Chitrita

Banerji's *Bengali Cooking*. The author herself is blessed with being thoroughly of what she writes, yet she can view her culture clearly from a distance and without loss of passion. The Bengali seasons and the events that usher them in and see them out are not like anything we know in North America or Europe – they are astonishingly new and strange. Chitrita Banerji's hands seek our heads and gently plunge us into the swirling waters of the most rich and amazing world of rivers and plains, fishes and festivals, culinary restrictions and celebrations, skies that are sultry and explosive by turns. We come up for air gasping with amazement, transformed by the seamless, graceful expression of the wholeness of a culture and the food that is born of it.

While Chitrita Banerji may hope to give her readers some authentic recipes to try at home, I wonder whether, paradoxically, she might not fail in her mission by the sheer force of her description of Bengali life. Once we taste the world from which these dishes come, we must sense the hopelessness of duplicating them, for – and this is the point this book so eloquently makes – food doesn't stand alone. What is *khichuri* without the joy and relief at the long-awaited monsoon and preceding oppressive humidity and hellish heat? Of course it is human to throw such considerations of the circumstances completely to the side and try to second guess. Thus even without the hope of monsoon coming to my semi-desert New Mexico neighborhood, I will be trying Chitrita's recipes for *khichuri* within the week. But as I savor this dish, I will be sobered when I recall the wealth of context that she provided, along with her instructions.

Bengali Cooking made me want to go immediately to Bengal to taste, smell, feel, and hear for myself everything that Chitrita describes. But it also made me wonder about my own culture and the context it provides for what we eat. Might it, in such skilful hands, have a comparable richness? It seems doubtful, but then perhaps I haven't opened my own eyes sufficiently wide to grasp my own history. This rich and wonderful book is indeed an eye-opener. Through its exquisite clarity about one life in a particular world, it raises questions about the possibilities for other worlds and reminds us that food is not separate from people, history, geography, and culture – in short, life itself.

Deborah Madison

INTRODUCTION

If you ask a Bengali for the shortest description of Bengali food, the answer is likely to be fish and rice, unless you are speaking to a vegetarian, in which case the answer may be greens and rice. If you are invited to someone's house for an elaborate, well-cooked meal that includes varieties of fish, vegetables and meat, not to speak of sweet dishes, your host will probably say, 'Do please grace my poor hovel with your presence and share our simple meal of *dal* and rice.' In this fertile tropical delta that serves as a basin for innumerable rivers, rivulets and tributaries, it is rice that has been the

common sustaining staple from pre-Aryan times until today.
Indeed, the commonest way of enquiring if a person has had
a meal, especially lunch, is to ask if he or she has taken rice.
Most people, if asked, will agree that a basic Bengali meal
will consist of rice, legumes, vegetables and fish.

But the minute you get into the details of cooking, a
startling polarisation of ideas and approach begins to emerge.
If you happen to talk to someone from West Bengal, a Ghoti,
you will probably be told that the uncivilised Bangals from
East Bengal know nothing about cooking, that they ruin food
by drowning it in oil and spices, that they eat half-cooked
fish, that even the best of fish can be ruined by their peculiar
habit of adding bitter vegetables to it. For their part, East
Bengalis will declare that Ghotis are the greatest philistines
on earth, who can cook nothing without making it cloyingly
sweet, that the freshest and most succulent of fish will be
reduced to leather by the way they fry it, that their miserliness
with spices renders all their dishes bland and colourless,
indeed that they are hardly even true Bengalis, because they
prefer to eat wheat-flour chapatis instead of rice at dinner.

If the warring culinary factions belong to the Hindu and
Muslim camps too, then you will also hear about the
shortcomings of the Muslim, who cannot cook without
onion and garlic and stinks of them himself, and of the Hindu
whose meat sauces are no better than cumin-flavoured water.
These jocular rivalries between Bengal on this or that side of
the border – or this or that side of the River Padma in the
days before partition – are likely to leave the newcomer
utterly bewildered, for initially the whole range of Bengali
food will seem broadly similar wherever you are.

But if you have the mind, the heart, the taste to explore,
you will find an enormous variety in a cuisine where richness
and subtlety are closely interwoven. With an array of
ingredients ranging from water lilies and potato and gourd
peel, to fish, meat, crab, tortoise and prawn, the Bengali has
also devised a combination of spices that is both ingenious
and delicate. From the simplest mashed potato enlivened

with mustard oil, green chillies or fried, crushed red chillies, raw onions and salt, to the exquisite prawn coated with spices and baked inside a green coconut, to the hilsa fish in mustard sauce, to the tantalising meat *rezala* made by Muslims – Bengalis take an equal delight in whatever they happen to have. By medieval times we already find in works of literature an extensive list of spices that includes turmeric, chillies, mustard, cloves, bay leaves, cardamoms, cinnamon, cumin, fennel, ginger, fenugreek, asafoetida and nutmeg. The variety of items is matched by a variety of cooking techniques despite the limitation of cooking being done on top of a stove. Vegetables are fried, boiled, roasted on a fire, combined with others and seasoned richly or lightly, or stir-fried with a pinch of whole spices which add their aroma to that of the vegetables. Fish can float in a most delicately suggestive thin stew (the *jhol*), can be made into a rich and spicy *kalia*, be fried crisply or be made into a self-contained *jhal*, red with ground chillies or yellow with ground mustard. Even the humblest of *dals* gains an unforgettable identity because of the *phoron* or flavouring added at the end. Every one of these items is eaten separately with a little bit of plain boiled rice. But even that plain rice has variety, depending on the size of the grains, the natural flavour of each species and whether it is parboiled or not.

The importance of such gourmet considerations to the Bengali can be measured by a political history written around 1788 by Sayyid Ghulam Husain Khan Tabatabai. In it he wrote that the Bengalis considered the people of Maharashtra uncivilised, not because the latter were continuously carrying out raids in Bengal and pillaging and torturing their victims, but for the unpardonable sin of not adding *phoron* to their *dal*! Similarly, a popular story goes that when the British shifted the capital of India from Calcutta to Delhi, those Bengali families who followed because of their work could easily be identified because smoke began to rise from their cooking fires at four in the morning and did not stop till midnight.

But the real food of Bengal, whether Hindu or Muslim, East or West, is not easy to reproduce on a mass scale, nor does it maintain its nuanced flavours after repeated heating or long hours in storage. Perhaps this explains the absence of a successful restaurant serving typical Bengali food in either West or East Bengal, despite the increasing urban trend of eating out. Most places tend to serve an imitation of northern Indian food, as do restaurants run by Bengali people settled in the US or the UK. Even in Dhaka, where Muslim meat dishes appear on the menu in many restaurants, the eating experience is seldom as satisfying as at somebody's house. I remember a restaurant called Pithaghar that bravely opened in Dhakar purporting to serve real Bengali delights like *pithas* and *khichuri* with *bhuna* duck. It did not survive. The kabab joints with their *nan* bread and varieties of kababs flourish, but there is hardly any difference between those in Dhakar and similar places in Delhi, Lucknow or Allahabad.

As a result, many outsiders, Indian and foreign, tend to conclude that there is no such thing as a Bengali cuisine, or that it is an extremely limited one. This is partly the fault of Bengalis themselves, for they cannot bring themselves to serve, much less flaunt, some of the simplest things which are also the best they have devised over time. No honoured guest nowadays is likely to be served plain potato *bharta*, or *begunpora*, or fried *matarshak* (leaves of the green pea), or the thinnest of fish *jhols*, redolent of *panch phoron* and with pieces of aubergines, potatoes and *boris* floating in it. These are the common daily items, and therefore not good enough for guests unless specifically requested. But they are also some of the best the region has to offer because they have been developed over centuries and are based on a meticulous selection of local ingredients. Even at very traditional Hindu weddings, say twenty years ago, the food was typically Bengali, but consisted only of the richer, spicier dishes.

The land of these food-loving characters, Bengal, is made up of the Indian state of West Bengal and the sovereign nation of Bangladesh (formerly East Bengal or East Pakistan), altogether an area of over 228,000 sq km (88,000 sq miles). Bangladesh has a population of 120 million and West Bengal of 80 million, so the Bengali nation is larger than most sovereign states, and Bengali comes a close sixth after the five major languages recognised by the United Nations. Most of the terrain is flat, delta land, criss-crossed with rivers, with a few hills and forests dotted here and there. Parts of the north are bordered by the Himalayas, and the western part of West Bengal is an extension of the rocky plateau of Chhotanagpur in the neighbouring state of Bihar. Overwhelmingly, though, this is a flat green land, most of it cultivated and divided into fields, primarily growing rice, the staple food crop. In the northern districts of Bangladesh and West Bengal the land is drier, a red laterite soil replacing the alluvial richness of the central areas. To the south, where Bengal slopes down to meet the Bay of Bengal, are the famous mangrove swamps, the Sundarbans, home of the Royal Bengal tiger and the huge *gharial* or Bengali crocodile. Like the rain forests of the Amazon delta or the Everglades in Florida (which they resemble in appearance), the Sundarbans are one of the few places where the mystery, beauty and terror of nature are still to be felt. Yet men can co-exist with nature, for these mangrove swamps are also home to a whole community of boat people who live by the catch they haul in from the Bay of Bengal.

The rivers of Bengal have served many purposes in sustaining life and prosperity. The great rivers – the Ganga, Padma, Meghna, Jamuna or Brahmaputra, Damodar, Ajoy, Tista, Karnaphuli and others – have always been conduits for goods moving from one place to another, while the Bay of Bengal has provided a natural entry for the incoming sea trade. Their fascination has been perennial, whether in the imagination of the poet or the mind of the ordinary peasant. Through the seasons their mood and appearance change dramatically. Attenuated in summer, they swell with life and energy during the monsoon rains and often become forces of destructive fury, only to be reduced to a tranquil fullness under an autumn sky. In winter the waters start shrinking, yielding the best possible catch of many kinds of fish for the food-lovers of Bengal.

Though the raging fury of a great river in flood during the height of the monsoon strikes terror in the hearts of the people, these same floods leave rich deposits of silt when they withdraw, replenishing the earth which has been over-cultivated. Sometimes shoals of land appear in the middle of the river, and people have fought and killed to acquire control over these extraordinarily fertile pieces of land. All of this has been conducive to a primarily agricultural way of life and to Bengal acquiring the reputation of a golden granary in later years. The rivers have also ensured the livelihood of the peasant, the boatman, the fisherman and the merchant, the most notable images of the Bengali people. In almost every folktale or fairy-tale, there are three young protagonists: the prince and his friends, the son of the chief constable and the son of the rich merchant. The merchant or trader, owner of a large fleet of trading ships travelling over the rivers and high seas, has also made his place in the medieval narrative poems of Bengal. The *Manasamangalkabya*, for instance, is centred around the figure of Chand Saudagar (merchant) who was a rigid follower of the god Shiva and refused to make his homage to Shiva's daughter Manasa, the snake goddess. She, in turn, plagued him with one disaster after another, including the death of his only beloved son Lakhindar, until peace was made by Chand's remarkable daughter-in-law Behula.

All the rivers, ponds, canals and lakes have contained a wealth of life. As the evidence of literature shows, fish has been part of life from ancient days to now. True, written evidence is scarce before the eleventh century, but as the historian Dr Nihar Ranjan Ray points out in his definitive text, *Bangalir Itihash*, the terracotta sculptures on the walls of Buddhist *viharas* in Paharpur and Moinamoti (now in Bangladesh), which go back to the days of the Pala and the Sena dynasty that ruled Bengal from the eighth to the eleventh centuries, provide reliable indications of lifestyle. Realistic portrayals show fish being cut, cleaned and transported in woven baskets. Nothing can be a greater testimonial to the continuity of food preference than to see the subsequent depiction of fish in folk art down the years. The nineteenth-century Kalighat *pats*, paintings, show an abundance of fish themes, of fisherwomen selling their goods in the market and of *babus* carrying their fishy purchases. Throughout the intervening years, the fish has figured as a motif in the quilts embroidered by Bengali women, in the *alpana* or decorative patterns drawn on floors or walls or seats, as a shape for home-made sweets and in innumerable proverbs and phrases. The eighteenth-century narrative poem *Annadamangalkabya*, by Bharatchandra, gives us a list of 51 varieties of fish that Bengalis ate in those days, and a food-loving poet in the nineteenth century, Iswarchandra Gupta, said that since Bengalis lived on fish and rice, nature had given them a land full of rice fields and rivers full of fish.

The greater part of this alluvial delta is eminently suitable for the cultivation of rice, and the planting, transplanting and harvesting of rice is the main activity of the Bengali peasant even today. There are three plantings every year, the major one, Aman, being planted during the monsoon and harvested in the late autumn. The Boro planting, a relatively modern practice made possible by improved irrigation techniques, takes place in winter, the crop being harvested in early summer. Immediately after that, around May-June, the least important Aush rice is planted to be harvested by late monsoon, around August-September. For main meals the Bengali tradition, in common with those of China, South-East Asia and the Pacific islands, is to eat plain boiled rice with vegetables and fish. It was not until the establishment of Islamic rule in India that pilaf, or *polao* as Bengalis call it, became a common item at feasts and banquets, the Muslim rulers, in keeping with the practice of the entire Middle Eastern region, finding it unpalatable to eat rice without first frying and then cooking it. In ancient and medieval times, Bengalis did, however, sometimes moisten their rice by pouring clarified butter, ghee, over it after it was served. A succinct description of an average person's meal can be found in the *Prakritapaingala*, written around 1400, in which there is a quotation from a hundred years earlier: 'Fortunate is the man whose wife serves him on a banana leaf some hot rice with ghee, mourala fish, fried leaves of the jute plant, and some hot milk on the side.'

The Bengali calendar year is a solar one based on the six seasons – two months for each – of Grishma, summer; Barsha, monsoon; Sharat and Hemanta, early and late autumn; Sheet, winter and Basanta, spring. The year begins with the month of Baisakh in mid-April, when the heat of the summer is on full blast. The whole landscape looks parched, the leaves on the trees start drooping and any cultivated plot that is not irrigated seems forlorn. Of course in terms of perceived temperatures and other natural manifestations, spring and summer overlap considerably. The heat of the summer is palpable even in March. The most important season in Bengal is Barsha, the monsoon, which lasts well into what is supposed to be early autumn. The torrential rains infuse the parched earth with new life and wash away the dust and grime of previous months. Everything glows with green vibrancy and the life-sustaining rice crop is planted, transplanted and lovingly nurtured throughout the season. Nothing can be more beautiful than stretches of emerald green rice fields under the slate-grey monsoon sky. The rivers assume their full majesty at this time, and rush along at full spate towards the sea. The autumn is a quiet time when the excessive moisture of the late monsoon starts to evaporate and the golden harvest stands ready in the fields. This is followed by the slow aridity of winter when balmy temperatures make the tropical delta a desirable resort.

The gentle rotation of the seasons, the garnering of the earth's resources and an active folk imagination have generated a large number of local rituals, some secular, which are indicated in the Bengali proverb of thirteen festivals in twelve months. Many of these are closely rooted in the soil and reflect a purely rural reality, even though some of them have survived into modern urban times. There are also the Muslim festivals based on a lunar calendar, which became part of Bengali life after the conversion of large numbers of people to Islam during medieval times. In a rotation parallel to the seasons, the two Ids, the fasting month of Ramzan, the 'Night of Destiny' and all other occasions touch the various calendar months in turn.

The memoirs of Huen Tsang, a seventh-century Chinese traveller who came to India to study at the centres of Buddhist learning, provide some indications of the food habits of those times. Onion and garlic were taboo items; the common items of food were rice, wheat, milk, sugar, mustard and some fish and meat. Onion and garlic did not become a part of the ordinary diet in Bengal until Muslim rule had become well-entrenched after the fourteenth century, and then, too, it was the local converts to Islam who accepted them. Hindus resisted until well into the nineteenth century. Not only did these two ingredients have heathen associations, they were also supposed to have a libidinous effect.

Huen Tsang mentioned only the elaborate feasts he attended in Bengal. Had he spent time in the hinterland, he would undoubtedly have listed fish and rice as the two foremost items in the local diet; Bengalis continued to subsist on them through the centuries, despite the advent of new influences, religious and political. Neither the disapprobation of non-violent Buddhism, nor the frowns of the vegetarian Brahmins of north or south India made any significant changes in the fish-loving Bengali's food habits. Brahmins all over India tended to be strict vegetarians until recently, and Bengali Brahmins were considered to be no better than heathens because of their weakness for fish. In desperation, some scholars in ancient Bengal like Bhavadeva Bhatta had to invent all kinds of specious justifications for including fish in the Brahmin's diet. Some scholars in medieval times even used to quote chapter and verse from the Sanskrit Puranas to demonstrate that fish was permissible except on certain religious occasions. Brahmins were let off with the half-stricture debarring them from eating certain kinds of fish, especially those of the eel variety, while large, scaly fish like carp were permissible food.

The abundance of fish also led to techniques for preserving excess supplies. Not content with sun-dried fish, in some areas Bengalis have also developed a taste for fermented fish. In Sylhet, where the huge lakes, *haors* and *baors*, are full of large, plump punti fish, people put them in earthen pots filled with mustard oil, seal the mouths and bury the pots underground. When they are taken out after a specific period, the fish has become an oily paste which is stored like a pickle. Little bits of it fried with chillies can be served as a relish with rice, or it can be put into a fresh fish stew to add its cheesy flavour.

But fresh or preserved, fish by itself would have no meaning for the Bengali. For the pleasure of savouring the taste of fish, he needed to have his portion of rice. The spectre of an empty larder with no rice is so dreadful to Bengalis that they cannot even bring themselves to articualte it. To indicate that the stock of rice is dwindling, the Bengali housewife says that the rice is 'increasing' – almost hoping to avert bad luck by the use of the opposite word. To the rural Hindu Bengali, rice is almost synonymous with Lakshmi, goddess of wealth and prosperity. Even today, many sophisticated urban Bengalis, who do not directly participate in the cultivation or processing of rice, find it irrationally difficult to waste a single grain. Even when the portion on the plate is too much, they will try to finish it because wasting rice is almost tantamount to insulting the goddess.

By medieval times Bengali literature began to contain elaborate descriptions of available and cooked food, thus unfolding a picture of a leisurely lifestyle among a certain class who loved good food and devised many elaborate and subtle ways of cooking it. Some of these texts list numerous kinds of fish most casually; I doubt if you can walk into any fish market in cities like Dhaka, Calcutta or Chittagong and find half that number on any given day. It is very noticeable that most of them were fresh-water rather than marine varieties. The preference still remains.

The dual entity of rice-fish which is at the heart of Bengali cuisine is reflected in a thousand and one ways in the rituals and ceremonies of the Bengali Hindus. Unhusked rice, called *dhan*, is an inevitable part of any ceremonial offering to the gods. In parts of West Bengal there is a custom that when a new bride arrives with her husband at his house, she is welcomed with a platter of offerings containing *dhan*. In her left hand she hold a live fish, which is later released into the family fishpond to breed and multiply. During the ceremony of eating the *shadh*, or desired foods, which takes place towards the end of pregnancy and is probably based on the assumption that if the mother has no unsatisfied cravings left she will produce a healthy child, rice and fish are the compulsory items. From the preferences of the living it is not such a big transition to the preferences of the dead. The spirits of ancestors are appeased at funerals by a final offering called the *pinda*, cooked rice and fish mixed together in a lump.

Apart from rice and fish, Bengalis have always taken advantage of the greens, vegetables and tubers that grow all over the land. Historians, basing their conclusions on a study of linguistics, think that modern vegetables like aubergines, several types of gourds and taro, as well as the bitterish leaves of the jute plant, figured in the pre-Aryan Bengali diet. The same goes for the indigenous fruits like *taal*, bananas, mangoes, jackfruits, coconuts and sugar-cane. Bananas were probably cultivated by the proto-Australoid peoples who originally inhabited the land. Both the fruit and the tree are abundantly represented in inscriptions and stone reliefs that date back to Bengal's antiquity. Like the rice plant, the banana tree also has a strong mythical significance in Bengali life. A young specimen is always placed outside the front door, together with a green coconut sitting atop an earthen pitcher, when a wedding or any other auspicious ceremony takes place. The same tree is pictured as the wife of Ganesa, elephant-headed god of success, son of the goddess Durga, Bengal's greatest deity. If a person dies on a Tuesday or a Saturday, the banana blossom has to be given as an offering.

Medieval poetry also gave its due to this tree. In the *Manasamangalkabya*, when the young and beautiful Behula finds herself widowed on her wedding night because of the malignancy of Manasa the snake goddess, she decides to win her husband back to life. Setting out all alone with her husband's corpse, she makes her momentous journey down the rivers to the underworld on a raft made from the trunks of banana trees. Every since, the saying 'crossing the ocean on a banana raft' has come to signify incredible or impossible feats based on faith and courage and little else.

One of the most striking differences of staple between ancient and contemporary times is the absence of any kind of pulses in the food of ancient Bengal. The earliest examples of Bengali literature, the *Charyapadas*, dating back approximately to the eleventh century, depict fishing and hunting for game, and mention rice, sugar-cane and many other crops, but there is no reference to any kind of *dal*. The first mention of *dal* and of ways of cooking it is in post-fifteenth-century literature. It seems that in this respect ancient Bengal had more in common with South-East Asia and China, where pulses are virtually unknown, than the Bengal of today. Even now, most of the *dals* consumed in West Bengal come from the other states in India. Apart from the natural cropping factor, the super-abundant supply of fish made *dal* as a source of protein unnecessary. The shift in balance in medieval times can probably be attributed to the spread of the Vaishnav Bhakti cult, whose followers were vegetarian. As a result, a substitute for fish or meat had to be found and the non-vegetarians also became familiar with this new element.

The relative scarcity of mustard, which has never been a

major crop in Bengal because it is not that well suited to the soil or climate, meant that the cooking medium was often ghee – clarified butter – instead of oil. Though it seems infinitely strange to modern Bengali cooks, for whom the main cooking medium is the pungent mustard oil, greens and vegetables were often fried in ghee in medieval times. As for rice, it was unthinkable to eat plain boiled rice without pouring ghee over it liberally, no matter how many other items there were. From the fourteenth century onwards we find many descriptions of hot, steaming rice, each grain unbroken, drenched in ghee which has given it a yellowish tinge. No wonder the prosperous ease-loving Bengalis found a little pot-belly the most natural of developments and aesthetically not unpleasing. Though we no longer fry green vegetables in ghee, it is still used in special preparations of vegetables like the *dalna* or the *ghanto*, as well as in rice preparations like *polao*, *khichuri* and *biryani* and the Muslim meat dishes. On occasion, even today, ghee will be poured over plain boiled rice if the first course consists of boiled or deep-fried vegetables.

In feudal Bengal ghee also acquired an elevated status as the preferred cooking medium for the wealthy. In nineteenth-century Calcutta many of the great feudal families would die rather than serve food cooked in mustard oil, which was considered fit only for the poor. There is an apocryphal story about an old lady from one of these families who fell sick on hearing that her nephew had taken to eating mashed potatoes flavoured with mustard oil – something that most Bengalis today would gobble up with relish.

A stable agricultural way of life also meant the presence of cattle. Milk and milk products became an important part of Bengali food from very early times. Apart from being drunk by itself, milk was often served at the end of a simple meal, when it was mixed with a little cooked rice and white sugar or date-palm sugar. In rural households nothing could be a more welcome symbol of plenty than the brown and white cows standing in their byres and the pitchers of foaming milk they produced. Even today, this symbolism remains in some houses in West Bengal. When the new bride arrives at her husband's house, her first step over the threshold is timed to coincide with the boiling over of a pot of milk in the kitchen.

Yoghurt, too, has been an important part of daily food, especially in the summer when it is thought to aid the digestion. Aryan culture attributed auspiciousness to it and Bengali Hindus continue to believe in that. A *tika* or dot is made on the forehead with yoghurt by well-wishing mothers or sisters whenever a child or sibling sets out on an important undertaking. Unsweetened yoghurt was used in cooking from fairly early times. The *Naishadhacharita*, probably written before the Hindu Sena dynasty took over in Bengal in the tenth century, mentions a dish, spiced with mustard and yoghurt and served at a royal wedding, which was apparently so hot that the guests had to shake and slap their heads. Muslims later used yoghurt as a substitute for wine. They also developed a drink called *borhani*, which is yoghurt mixed with water and whipped together with salt and ground black pepper. This continues to be served even today at Muslim feasts at which a lot of rich meats and *polaos* are supposed to be digested with the aid of the *borhani*. Many of their meat dishes require a little marinading in yoghurt, and the *korma* and the *rezala* in Bangladesh are both based on a yoghurt sauce. As for the Bengali Hindus, some of their classic fish and vegetable dishes are cooked in a yoghurt sauce.

The most sophisticated transmutation of milk in Bengal has been in the form of infinitely varied sweets, some made at home and some professionally. Certainly, no other region in India has shown such passionate absorption in sweets and appreciation of subtlety or variety in their preparation. The plump Bengali with his sweet tooth takes seriously the ancient Sanskrit recommendation, *madhurena samapayet* – a meal should be finished with something sweet – to the heights of finicky epicureanism. The Aryan tradition of central India gave us rice pudding and *kheer* or evaporated milk. To this the Bengali added his repertoire of sweet *pithas*, made with rice or wheat flour, coconut, milk, even pasted *dal*, and sweetened with sugar or *gur* from the date-palm tree; he was content with this for many centuries.

Despite warring kings in pre-medieval times and successive Muslim conquests by Turks, Arabs and Afghans from the thirteenth to the mid-sixteenth century, when the emperor Akbar made Bengal a part of his Moghul empire, the prosperity of Bengal regmained unchanged, as did her social and economic inequalities. So great was her income from a flourishing export trade that even at the tail-end of Moghul rule the entire imperial army was sustained exclusively by the revenue sent by this province to the Delhi treasury. It was during the fourteenth century, when Bengal was under the Turkish sultan Ilyas Shah that the entire region came to be commonly referred to as *Bangla* or Bengal.

Literary evidence from before the tenth century reflects the wide disparity between the diets of the rich and the poor. While ordinary people ate plain rice with a little fish and vegetables and some milk, it was common for the affluent to serve elaborate meals, especially at weddings and other festive occasions. The feast served at the wedding of the princess Damayanti, as described in the *Naishadhacharita*. included so many dishes that guests could not keep track of what they ate; nor, even, could they sample every dish. Venison, goat meat and gamebirds were served, as were fish and vegetable preparations, some of which were cleverly made to resemble meat. For sweet dishes there were many kinds of *pithas* and the inevitable sweet yoghurt. But the only drink served was water. Finally, the guests were served *paan*, betel leaves wrapped around sweet spices. These basics of a festive menu did not change for many centuries.

Much later, during the medieval period of Bengali history, when the *mangalkabyas*, narrative poems, as well as a lot of Vaishnav poetry and biography were written, we begin to find Bengalis sitting down to fairly elaborate meals at home even when there is no festivity. A Bengali phrase refers to the

66 dishes which made up a proper banquet. This figure is probably based on several centuries of an elaborate eating tradition in which the male was a god, the woman his cook and servitor and the rice on the centre of a huge platter was surrounded by individual bowls containing a variety of items. There was no tradition of men and women eating together. The males of every household had the right to sit down first and eat the best and the most. This practice can be seen all the way down the caste and class scales. Even in a very poor peasant family in Bangladesh where the menu is minimal, the man is served by the woman. The wife, mother or daughter-in-law would have to sit in front, her face half-covered with her sari, and observantly offer to serve extra helpings whenever needed.

Hindu widows in Bengal were forced to go on a vegetarian diet for as long as they lived, a cruel stricture rigidly enforced by their families. One explanation for this could be the equally cruel supposition that these poor creatures, often still in their youth, were considered potentially troublesome charges. They were not allowed to remarry, and one false step into temptation would bring shame to the entire family. So a deficient diet and other hardship were indirect ways of despatching them to the next world, sometimes to the pecuniary advantage of their in-laws. But not all widows were obliging enough to drop dead fast. They lived and did their share of the drudgery, particularly in the kitchen. Tradition ascribes to these women, who made the best of a bad bargain, the excellence, range and subtlety of Hindu vegetarian cooking in Bengal. A noted food writer of the nineteenth century is supposed to have quipped that it was impossible to taste the full glory of vegetarian cooking unless your own wife became a widow.

The long period of Muslim rule from the eleventh century to the demise of the Moghul empire and the take-over by the British in the mid-eighteenth century firmly established Islam as the second most important religion of Bengal. Mass conversions took place from the lower castes of Hindu society whose members had been oppressed and exploited by the higher castes under the well-entrenched forces of orthodox Brahminism. The remnants of the Buddhists who had surved the tyranny of aggressive Hinduism under the Sena dynasty were also tempted to accept the faith of the Muslim rulers. This process continued until by the latter half of the nineteenth century Muslims constituted almost half the population of Bengal. In northern and eastern Bengal they were the majority, but they had little besides their strength of numbers. Land, power, good education and professional opportunities were reserved for the Hindu élite. This inequality and geographical concentration sowed the seeds of discontent which eventually led to East Bengal becoming East Pakistan when the Indian subcontinent gained independence in 1947. But with inequality and disaffection continuing to be the lot of Bengali Muslims within Pakistan, they decided to break away in the hope of a better future. The birth of Bangladesh in 1971, after a bitter war of liberation, created another South Asian nation-state, but popular expectations of prosperity and social equality have remained substantially unfulfilled.

Culinarily, the impact of Muslim cooking was at first mostly to be seen among the leisured and affluent classes, especially the Nawabs who represented the Moghul empire in Bengal. However restricted this was initially, it led to the development of a Bengali Muslim cuisine which is distinctly different from the Moghul cuisine of northern India and the Nizami cooking of Hyderabad. Bengali cuisine is less rich and more subtle than either of these, tending to substitute yoghurt and lemon juice for the cream and solid *kheer* of other Muslim cooking. Beef and chicken were also introduced into the diet; the former a bitter bone of contention even today, the latter becoming a part of Hindu households. Onion and garlic too, became commonly used ingredients in Muslim households, even the poorest ones. By the nineteenth century the prejudiced Hindu image of the Muslim was of a character reeking of those two alliums. One of the best-known specialities developed by the Bengali Muslims is the *rezala* made with *khashi* or castrated goat, in which lemon, yoghurt, milk and spices are combined with the almost heretical addition of lots of hot green chillies. Fragrant and sharp, the chillies produce an uplifting sensation for a palate cloyed with an excess of ghee or other ground spices.

The taste of many kinds of *polaos, biryanis*, kababs and the *parota* bread Bengal also owes to the Muslims. The last, made with a flour dough and fried in ghee, can mean many things to many people. The average Bengali household, Hindu or Muslim, will serve a flat three-cornered piece of fried bread and call it a *parota*. In others, where the cook or the hostess takes pride in her art, a circular *parota* of five or six layers will be served, but if you are dealing with a first-class Muslim cook or *baburchi*, he can present you with a de luxe circle the size of a small dinner plate, with fifty or sixty flaky layers underneath a golden-brown surface. Rich and heavy though it is, this *Dhakai parota*, as it came to be known all over Bengal, eaten with judiciously chosen meat dishes, definitely justifies a trip to Bangladesh.

It must be remembered, though, that these sophisticated meat, rice and wheat dishes did not develop immediately after the Muslims came to Bengal. The sultans who preceded Moghul rule were no patrons of local culture. They were far more interested in battles against local rivals, profit and self-aggrandisement than in creating a stable environment for the development of the fine arts. Though they and their followers made meat a major part of their diet, the cooking methods probably remained confined to the simple techniques of grilling and roasting over open fires. The sophistication so evident in fish and vegetable recipes did not come to meat cooking for a long time. Even under the emperor Akbar, who ensured peace and stability in Bengal, the food-loving poets of the *mangalkabyas* make no mention of the *rezala, korma, bhuna* or *biryani* that is trotted out at weddings in Bangladesh today.

The last Nawab of Bengal lost his throne and his life after

the Battle of Plassey in June 1757, but the two centuries of British presence in Bengal did not really make much difference to the way urban or rural Bengal continued to eat. In common with the rest of India, the colonial presence resulted in an Anglo-Indian cuisine which remained confined by and large to the ruling race and the mixed breed of Anglo-Indians. The one noticeable contribution this has made to everyday Bengali food is the inclusion of two extraordinary misnomers, chop and cutlet. These English words, which have now become Bengali, were probably adopted by the cooks who worked in British households to denote their crossbreed concotions. The chop today means a round or oval potato cake with a fish or meat stuffing, which is dipped in egg and breadcrumbs, then fried crisply. The cutlet, which can be meat, chicken or prawn, usually means one of those elements seasoned lightly and pounded to form a long, flat oval, which is then coated and fried the same way, the prawn tail or a piece of bone sticking out at one end like a trademark device. From the *baburchi*'s kitchen it did not take long for these two items to end up in urban eating joints, and there are many shops in Bengali towns that specialise in 'chop-cutlet' as a genre. Vegetarian versions of both have also developed, but the mustard that is inevitably served with these is not the Colman's mustard favoured by the British, but Bengali *kasundi*, a palate-blowing mixture of pungent mustard paste, mustard oil, lemon juice or sour green mango, traditionally served with greens or bitter gourds and rice.

Restaurants and guest-houses in Bengal also have pretentious 'English' menus where a pallid 'roast' drenched in Worcestershire or tomato sauce is flanked on the plate by shrivelled fried potatoes and lackadaisical boiled vegetables – a sad reminder of the recent past. The only overwhelming British tradition we have developed, in common with many other races, is that of tea-drinking. However, the first time on record when a Bengali drank tea was probably when the renowned Buddhist scholar Atish Dipankar Srignan went to Tibet in the eleventh century at the invitation of the king to

propagate Buddhist teachings in Tibet, and he would
certainly have drunk Chinese green tea.

The innovative genius of the Bengali cook, both Hindu and
Muslim, has found expression in modern times in an amazing
array of sweets, most of them based on milk. The concept of
pithas being synonymous with sweets is now an archaic one.
Instead there are the *sandesh*, the *rosogolla*, the *pantua*, the
chamcham, or the *rosomalai* to be enjoyed. All of these are
made, fully or partly, with *chhana*, the solid part of curdled
milk. These *chhana* sweets are Bengal's contribution to the
Indian universe of sweets. In other parts of India, sweets are
either of the *halva* variety or based on *kheer* thick enough to
be solidified. This is probably because for a long time people
there believed that 'cutting' the milk with acid to make
chhana is a sin. Krishna, whose idyllic pastoral childhood
among the cowherds of Brindaban has been the subject of
such a large body of poetry in central and northern India, is
depicted as a mischievous boy stealing butter and cream, but
never *chhana*.

This passion for *chhana* and its offspring is something very
recent in the history of Bengali eating. Even in the
mid-nineteenth century there is no mention of *sandesh* or
rosogolla, today the twin pillars of Bengal's sweet repute. The
eminent Bangladeshi historian, Professor Abdul Razzaque, is
convinced that there was no domestic midwifery in the birth
of these sweets. They were probably devised by the
professional sweet-makers in the markets during the latter
half of the nineteenth century, which is probably why they
continue to be mostly made in shops rather than at home.
Over the last fifty years, famous sweet shops have risen and
fallen in the cities of Dhaka and Calcutta, and each in its
heyday has been famous for one or two particular products.
The *sandesh* from Bhim Chandra Nag, the *rosogolla* from
K. C. Das (whose father Nabin Chandra Das is supposed to
be its creator), the *mishti doi* from Jalojoga, are all
indications of the importance of the *moira*, professional
sweet-maker, in Bengali society.

Tradition pictures the *moira* as a huge, immobile mountain of flesh, sitting either in front of his stove or of a huge platter of white *chhana* which he manipulates with the ease of long practice. He is utterly oblivious to all else in the world and so satiated with his own products that he never touches them any more. Not all *moiras*, of course, are embalmed in a sugary stupor. The great Bhim Chandra Nag was once challenged by Lady Canning, the then Vicereine of India, to create a new sweet for her birthday. In response, the master craftsman invented something which is neither the *pantua* (akin to the *golapjamun* served in Indian restaurants everywhere), nor the *langcha*, a similar, bolster-shaped creation. This new product, large, spherical, succulent and fragrant, became known as the *ladikanee* after its patron, Lady Canning. While many shops make them today, the Bhim Nag *ladikanee* is still considered special.

What a Bengali eats today is determined as much by his means as by his personal preference. For the very poor, it has always been a struggle to get even an adequate supply of the basic rice. The image of empty cooking pots keeps recurring in Bengali literature from the eleventh-century *Charyapadas* to medieval lamentations by Phullara, wife of the hunter Kalketu, down to modern Bengali fiction. Many poor peasants in Bangladesh remain content daily with just rice, an onion or two, some chillies and the handful of *shak* or boiled potato. Urban workers living in slums often feel lucky if they can manage a regular supply of rice and *dal*. Ironically, if such people do happen upon a bit of fish, they cannot even enjoy that for want of fuel or the oil to cook it. During the recent famines – 1943 in all of Bengal, when an estimated 2 million people died, 1974 in Bangladesh – the skies have echoed with tormented voices begging only for some *phan*, the starchy gruel drained out from the rice.

Even without such stark conditions, there is bound to be a marked contrast between the food of the very rich and the very poor, as everywhere in the world. But throughout history there has always been an intermediate group – landed gentry, prosperous peasants, merchants, businessmen, middle-class professionals – that has managed to eat well, with variety of taste and material, and without having to spend huge sums on food. The nineteenth-century figure of fun and comedy, the plump, sleek, indolent, pleasure-loving Bengali *babu*, is a product of many centuries of such gustatory gratification. And over the course of a lifetime, his eating experiences have been like the beautifully soft quilts the womenfolk have made during their leisure hours out of torn old saris. Some of these were very plain, only a criss-cross grid of stitches holding them together, but aesthetically pleasing because of the woven borders or motifs on the original saris. Then there were the others, the *nokshikanthas*, patterned quilts, which were works of art. Some of them took a lifetime to complete and displayed the most exquisite and complex designs in subtly graded colours, but always using the same simple stitch and always based on everyday life and reality. The hand of the artist plied the needle in and out of the quilted cloth and the stitches fell so fine that they were hard to make out individually.

In the kitchen the same artist's hand would throw together the simplest of spices and use the most humble everyday ingredients in cooking meals for the whole family. But despite the simplicity, this taste of Bengal remains hard to define, quantify, memorise and reproduce, though easy to recall with nostalgic longing. It delights with nuances and suggestions. But like the fabled golden deer, it will elude outsiders until they decide to take the risk of bridging all distance, to enter, observe, feel and absorb Bengal. The encounter, depending on its intensity, is bound to bring both euphoric revelations and sharp let-downs, but I believe that for the truly adventurous an initial exploration simply serves as a beckoning invitation to many more.

EATING AND SERVING BENGALI FOOD

The Bengali people are perhaps the greatest food lovers in the Indian subcontinent. A leisurely meal of many items which requires long hours of labour and ingenuity in the kitchen has long been as much a part of Bengali culture as ceremonial eating in France. The traditional way of serving food is on the floor, where individual pieces of carpet, called *asans*, would be spread for each person to sit on. In front of this seat would be placed a large platter, made of bell metal or silver depending on the family's economic status. Around this platter would be arrayed a number of small metal or silver bowls in which portions of *dal*, vegetables, fish, meat, chutney and dessert would be served. In the centre of the platter there would be a small mound of piping hot rice flanked by vegetable fritters, wedges of lime, whole green chillies and perhaps a bit of pickle. Finally, in the centre of the mound a little hole would be made to pour in a spoonful of ghee or clarified butter to flavour the initial mouthfuls of rice.

The star of the eating scene was inevitably the male: husband, father, son, son-in-law and others. The women would hover around, anxiously serving extra helpings or directing the servants to bring them. Some of the women would sit and ply palm-leaf fans to cool the heated male brow as the pleasures of intake intensified, but in traditional homes there would always be the secondary meal when the women could finally sit down and enjoy their meal. True, the best portions of fish and meat would be gone, devoured by the superior sex, but that did not detract significantly from their enjoyment. The long-established female tradition of savouring the ultimate pleasure from concoctions of vegetables and fishbones or succulent stalks cooked with tiny shrimps or various kinds of pickles and chutneys is rooted in this practice of making the best of secondary resources.

The approach to food is essentially tactile. As in all of India, Bengalis eat everything with their fingers. Neither table silver nor chopsticks are used as aids to convey food to the mouth. What, after all, could be better than one's own sensitive fingers to pick out the treacherous bones of fish like hilsa or koi? Quite apart from this functional aspect, the fingers also provide an awareness of texture which becomes as important as that felt by the tongue. The various mashed vegetables or the different kinds of rice or varieties of fish we eat are all appreciated by the fingers before they enter the mouth.

Each individual has a particular style of dealing with his or her food. Some people pick up their rice and accompaniments very daintily, their fingers barely touching the food. This is supposed to be the style of the élite. Others prefer to mash their rice in their fingers before mixing it with the other items. Yet others will form balls of rice and other items in their palms before popping it in their mouths. Children are inevitably fed this way by their mothers. Then there are those hearty, somewhat coarse eaters who can be seen licking their palms all the way to their wrists and 'Up to one's wrist in food' has become a Bengali phrase to denote gluttonous indulgence. The other peculiarity about the Bengali eating scene is the unashamed accumulation of remnants. Since succulent vegetable stalks, fish bones and fish heads, meat and chicken bones are all meticulously chewed until not a drop of juice is left inside, heaps of chewed remnants beside each plate are an inevitable part of a meal. The custom of immediately and scrupulously wiping clean the part of the floor – now the table – where food has been eaten is probably related to the presence of such remnants.

Whether you have five dishes or sixty, the most important part of eating in Bengal is eating each dish separately with a little bit of rice in order to savour its individual bouquet. Not for the Bengali an indiscriminate mixing of fish, meat, *dal* or vegetables together with the rice in one graceless huddle, as outsiders tend to do in Indian restaurants at home or abroad. Any cook who takes pride in his or her art feels outraged at this kind of tasteless mixing of food. The more delicate tastes always come first and it is only by graduating from these to the stronger ones that you can accommodate the whole range of taste. Vegetables, especially the bitter ones, are the first items followed by *dal*, perhaps accompanied by fries or fritters of fish and vegetables. After this comes any of the complex vegetable dishes like *ghanto* or *chachchari*, followed by the important fish *jhol* as well as other fish preparations. Meat will always follow fish, and chutneys and *ambals* will provide the refreshing touch of tartness to make the tongue anticipate the sweet dishes. Of course, modern daily food is limited to only one vegetable, one *dal* and either fish or meat, but the order remains the same.

Basanta · Grishma
SPRING AND SUMMER

Flagrantly scarlet on bare branches or covertly crimson amidst dark green foliage, the early flowers of spring arrive to signal an end to the mellow contentment of winter and to herald a brief unsettling season. Hardly perceived before it is over, spring in Bengal combines beauty and terror like the longer-lasting monsoon. The variety of colours ranged on the trees and the fragrance of mango trees in blossom carried by the balmiest of evening breezes create a lightness of being

before the relentless weight of summer sets in. A little later in
the season the heady scent of gardenia in the evenings
heightens sensory awareness to a new pitch, but the
changeable weather of spring is inevitably accompanied by
outbreaks of chickenpox and measles. Not so long ago a
greater terror stalked the land at this time: smallpox, whose
Bengali name, Basanta, is synonymous with the season itself.

According to the Bengali calendar, the two months of
Falgun and Chaitra, mid-February to mid-April, are to be
counted as the spring. By the end of March, however, one can
already feel the cruelty of the summer sun and the long, dusty
wait for the monsoon starts as moisture evaporates from leaf
and land while a humid haze covers the sky.

Food in a Bengali household takes on the summer pattern
fairly early in the spring. Daytime temperatures are hot
enough for the traditional housewife to buy and serve 'cool'
items to her family. This belief in the hot and cold quality of
foods has been a fundamental part of local beliefs for a long
time, probably dating back to theories of indigenous
Ayurvedic medicine developed under the Aryans. The
Charakasamhita, an Ayurvedic text written by Charaka
around the first century BC, contains detailed descriptions of
the specific attributes of foods as well as detailed instructions
on eating and keeping healthy. Having been a great drinker
himself, Charaka extolled the virtues of alcohol, but this part
of his teaching has not taken root in Bengal. Nor has his
stricture against the consumption of fish and milk together,
on the grounds that they would burden the digestive system.

But the belief in the specific attributes of different foods has
continued to flourish here because of a long tradition of
Ayurvedic medicine practised by local physicians. Even now,
women of my mother's generation will serve vegetables like
lau, white gourd, or okra or *patol*, the small striped gourd
known as *parwal* in other parts of India, during the summer,
convinced that these will keep the body cool. Meat, eggs,
onions and garlic, on the other hand, are studiously avoided.
Ginger, though, is encouraged because it is believed to

increase the appetite and aid digestion if taken before meals
with a little salt. As for biliousness, which seems to have been
a universal affliction in the old days, Ayurvedic practitioners
will recommend *patols*, cucumbers and the two varieties of
bitter gourd, *karola* and *uchchhe*.

The association of healthy properties with a bitter taste
and the subsequent appreciation of that bitterness as a taste is
a Bengali peculiarity that outsiders find incomprehensible.
Even for the natives, it is an acquired taste. Most children,
including myself in my pre-teen schooldays, recoil from these
bitter vegetables. My mother, a determined woman, would
force me to swallow bitter gourds, leaves of the *neem* or
margosa tree, and a *shukto* made with mixed vegetables and
the excruciatingly bitter leaves of the *patol*, even though tears
rolled down my face. Years of force-feeding accomplished the
intended miracle, for nothing tastes sweeter now than the
bitter vegetables served with rice at the beginning of a meal.

My personal favourite is the simple *neembegun*, made with
aubergines cut into small cubes and fried with a handful of
the bitter *neem* leaves. In the spring coppery new leaves cover
the branches and are ideal for making this dish, being slightly
less bitter than the older leaves. The virtues of the *neem* are
supposed to be many. Its oil is extracted to be made into
beneficial soap, its twigs are broken off and chewed at the
ends to make fibrous natural toothbrushes in rural areas. But
the greatest of its medicinal properties is to be seen during the
rampaging outbreaks of chickenpox. When the scabs dry and
the whole body is one gigantic agonising itch, *neem* leaves are
boiled in water and used to sponge the patient to give
exquisite relief. Sometimes, soft branches are tied together
and used like an improvised brush to rub the patient's body.

The bitter gourds, *karola* and *uchchhe*, are not confined to
the spring and the summer. In our house they are
year-round favourites and can be eaten boiled and
mashed, or sliced and fried crisp, or made into a soft
chachchari with sliced potatoes, ground mustard and a little
panch phoron. But their real glory emerges in *shukto*, the

strange preparation in which Bengalis take such pride. The term is derived from the medieval Bengali *shukuta*, meaning the dried leaves of a plant, usually the bitter jute plant. These leaves were stored throughout the year and used to make a bitter dish with seasonal vegetables. From the mythical Shiva in the narrative poems to the historical figure of Chaitanya, medieval Bengalis loved *shukto*, and all the more so because it was believed to be an antidote for excessive mucus in the gut, a sign of dysentery.

The *shukto* remains one of the best instances of a Hindu Bengali cook's ingenuity, with a combination of subtle half-tones rather than any dominant taste. The bitterness is rarely allowed to overpower the other flavours, which include the sharpness of mustard, the grainy blandness of poppy seeds and the caramelly flavour of ghee. In the old days no woman was considered a good cook unless she could produce a creditable *shukto*: a nursery rhyme in my childhood heaped ridicule on a poor girl called Rani because she knew so little that she had put hot chillies in her *shukto* and flavoured her sour *ambal* with ghee. Of course, there are the fifth columnists who declare that *shukto* is a superb instance of the Bengali's low cunning, for anything you serve after a bitter item is bound to taste wonderful.

Whatever the motives for serving *shukto*, it is an integral part of summer menus, regularly served to guests on formal occasions, even as late as twenty years ago, and with infinite variations. The vegetables may vary according to season and availability, with the characteristic bitter taste produced either by the bitter gourds, or by the leaves of the *patol* or by some other leafy green. Ethnic shops outside India now sell bitter gourds, so the adventurous cook can easily try this recipe.

 We often feel you cannot have too much of **Shukto**. For four people we usually take about 500 g (1 lb) of cubed or sliced mixed vegetables such as potatoes, aubergines, sweet potatoes, green papayas, local radishes, flat beans, green bananas, *patols*, ridged gourd or *jhinge* and, of course,

bitter gourds. In the West some of these will not be
available, but one can substitute any firm vegetable for
these and whatever gourds happen to be around (squash or
courgettes can be tried, though pumpkin is too sweet). The
thing to remember is that the bitter gourds should be sliced
very fine and should not be more than one fifth of the total
quantity of vegetables. Once all the vegetables have been
washed, heat a little oil in a *karai* and sauté the bitter gourd
slices for three to four minutes. Remove and keep apart.
Add a little more oil to the pot (the total amount should be
about 2 tablespoons) and throw in ½ teaspoon of *panch
phoron*. A couple of minutes later, add the rest of the raw
vegetables, stir for four to five minutes and add enough
water to cook the vegetables. Keep covered until they are
cooked, add the fried bitter gourds together with salt to
taste and 3 teaspoons sugar. Cook over a high heat for
another three to four minutes and remove from the stove.

To spice this dish we use 1 tablespoon of ground *posto*
or poppy seeds (again, available in ethnic shops), 3
tablespoons of mustard seeds (ground fine with a touch of
salt) and 1 tablespoon of ground ginger. This is added in
the second stage of the cooking, when 1 tablespoon of oil is
heated in another pot, and another ½ teaspoon of *panch
phoron*, together with 2 bay leaves and half the ground
ginger thrown into it. Once this has been fried for a minute
or so, the cooked vegetables with the gravy are poured in
and brought to the boil. The *posto* and mustard are
combined in a bowl with 2 teaspoons of flour and a little
water and the paste is added to the pot. After cooking these
for three to four minutes, 2 teaspoons of ghee and the rest
of the ginger are added. The salt and the sugar are checked,
the whole thing stirred thoroughly to blend the flavours
and the pot removed from the fire. The sweetness should
balance the bitterness, so more sugar might be needed. It is
up to the cook to decide how much sugar he or she wants
to add; being Ghotis, we like our *shukto* to be sweetish,
but others prefer it more bitter. The sauce should be thick,
not watery, and whitish in colour. I find that the delicacy of
flavour is heightened if the *shukto* is served warm rather
than piping hot.

When *shukto* is not possible, the Bengali passion for bitterness finds expression in the addition of bitter vegetables to *dal*. There is both variety and a strict order in the cooking and serving of *dals*. Three or four different types can be served at the same meal, especially among the Hindus of East Bengal. You can start with a bitter *dal* with vegetables, then, after one or two separate vegetable dishes you can have a roasted *moong dal* cooked with a fish head. Finally, after the fish and the meat but before the chutney and dessert, a sour *dal*, made either with green mangoes or tamarind or any other sour fruit like the star fruit, can be served. Such elaborate meals are rare now, but a surprising variety of *dals* is still part of the Bengali cook's daily repertoire. The proverbial phrase 'poor man's rice and *dal*' can easily be made into a far from poor meal.

The most important thing about cooking *dal* is the *phorons* or spices used for flavouring it. Different *dals* will have different combinations for *phorons* and the same *dal* can have several different *phorons*, depending on the mood of the cook. The first step for all *dals*, though, is always the same: boiling in water until it is soft and soupy, the amount of water needed varying widely, depending on how thin or how thick you want your *dal* to be. My family thought of lentils as a rather thick potage with long, slices of onion and green chillies and, of course, a sweetish undertaste, so when I first went to live in Bangladesh with my husband, I was very disconcerted at seeing the thin *dal* that appeared on my in-laws' table. The taste was different too, for the lentils had been flavoured with minutely chopped onions and garlic, together with bay leaves and dried red chillies, all fried in oil.

In summer the common *dals* in our home are *moong* and *kalai* rather than lentils, yellow split peas or pigeon peas. And while in winter the *moong dal* may be roasted in a frying pan before cooking, in summer it is preferred *kancha* or unroasted, because it is easier to digest and does not heat the system.

For **Kancha moong dal** for four people, take 250 g (½ lb) of *moong dal* and rinse it in a colander under running water three to four minutes. Somehow, this makes a difference even if the *dal* is clean. As you hold the *dal* under water, squeeze it in handfuls to make sure that the surface dust is thoroughly washed off. Heat 750 ml (1¼ pints) of water in a pot. When it comes to the boil, add the *dal* and a teaspoon of salt. If you wish, you can also add a teaspoon of turmeric powder. When the *dal* is cooked, remove from the stove. Take a small piece of ginger, enough to make 2 teaspoonsful, and chop it fine. Heat 1½ teaspoons of oil in a *karai* or frying pan and throw in 2 dried red chillies. When they turn black, add 1 teaspoon of whole mustard seeds. As soon as these stop sputtering, add the ginger and 2 bay leaves. Stir for a minute, add 1 teaspoon of ghee and pour the *dal* over it. Taste for salt, add a little sugar, keep on a high flame for three to four minutes and remove. The thickness of the *dal* can be suited to your taste. You can change the amount of water.

The same *dal*, once it has been boiled, can be treated a little differently. Before removing the cooked *dal*, add 1 tablespoon of juice of freshly ground ginger and 2–3 green chillies. Then heat some oil separately, fry 2 bay leaves, the ginger pulp from which the juice was pressed and 1 teaspoon of *panch phoron* in it. Pour the *dal* over this, cook for three to four minutes, taste and remove.

Though the *kancha moong dal* is such a summer favourite, sometimes my mother would make an equally simple version of *masoor dal*, lentils. This dal, for some odd reason, is considered non-vegetarian by the Hindus and therefore forbidden to widows. Its usual recipe with onions is more suitable to the cooler temperatures of monsoon and winter, but this particular recipe, somehow, made it past all apprehensions of heat and appeared in summer. I have no idea how my mother came by this recipe, but I have never had it anywhere else.

The **Masoor dal** – again 250 g (½ lb) is enough for four – is boiled in 750 ml (1¼ pints) of water with salt. Then, instead of any *phoron* being fried separately, 1 tablespoon of good ghee and 2 green chillies chopped very fine are dropped into the *dal*. It is left covered for five minutes to let the flavours mingle and tastes so good that the absence of *phoron* is not noticed.

Once, in Dhaka, a good friend of mine, Salma Sobhan, was talking to me about Muslim Bengali cooking. She explained that among its intricacies were a few simple dishes, like lemon *dal*, that amazed one with their taste. What was that, I asked, and she was taken aback at such ignorance.

For **Lemon dal** it is the same *kancha moong dal* that is used. Once cooked with a little salt and water, it is sieved through a cheesecloth so that it comes out as a thick, creamy soup, without the fibres. Then a large porcelain or earthenware (never metal) serving bowl is taken and the bottom and sides lined with thin slices of lemon or lime. Bengalis prefer to use the fragrant *kagaji* or *gondhi* lemon, if they are available. Once the slices are in place, the sieved *dal* is put back on the stove, brought to the boil and kept there for two to three minutes, then poured into the lemon-lined basin and kept covered for about five minutes to absorb the taste and flavour of the lemon. This needs to be served with plain rice, preferably an *atap* (non-parboiled) rice like Basmati. The problem with this *dal* is that it can neither be reheated, nor kept overnight, for it tends to turn bitter. To serve it for guests, cook and sieve it earlier, then boil and pour it over the lemons just before serving.

Despite all considerations of health and cool foods in summer, Bengalis do, on special occasions, indulge their taste for rich and spicy concoctions. This is true of *dal* too.

One of the great Bengali classics *muror dal*, cooked with a fish head and strong spices, was often served at weddings and feasts even at the height of summer. In our family, my mother's third sister, whom I called Aunt from Shyambajar (in north Calcutta), was absolutely crazy about it and was quite prepared to give up all fish, meat, vegetable or dessert items for the pleasure of eating her fill of *muror dal*!

Though the days are filled with a dry heat, the aridity of summer is still far away. The fields look dry, but not parched, and the new green leaves on the trees still retain some of their clean glow. In the gardens the smell of gardenias during the day is matched by the less powerful though no less heady fragrance of the first *kamini* flowers and of the bell-shaped golden champak. The mango blossoms are replaced by tiny budding mangoes and the long leaves of the lychee trees try unsuccessfully to hide the clusters of new-born lychees. One of the most beautiful trees is the tamarind, whose tiny feathery leaves in fan-like formations wave enticingly in the breeze. A Bengali proverb uses the smallness of an individual tamarind leaf as a metaphor for adjustability: if good men are together, even nine of them will manage to find space to sit on a single tamarind leaf. Among the strangest sights of this short spring is the huge *shojne* or *shajina* tree. These bear elongated pods in spring, but unlike the tamarind, the *shojne* pods are about 30 cm (1 ft) long and look like ribbed stems. The colonial British called them drumsticks and the appearance is the obvious reason behind its misnomer in Bengali, *shojne danta*, the word *danta* meaning a succulent stalk. Bunches of this firm, fleshy, chewy and short-lived vegetable are sold at high prices in the markets in springtime. They are also added to *machher jhol*, fish stew, which is the centrepiece of the Bengali lunch all through the summer.

The *jhol* can be cooked in a hundred different ways, but its frequent appearance in the menu has made it the most well-known Bengali dish. It is a thin stew, usually of fish, though it can also be purely vegetarian. But the fish in a *jhol* is always combined with vegetables. Though several different ground spices are used in cooking *jhol*, a good one's most important quality is its lightness. Too heavy a hand with the spices will ruin it. At the same time, bad cooks can also produce watery, tasteless, pallid *jhols*. Achieving the right balance only comes with much practice. But good or bad, the *jhol* is the most important item in the Bengali lunch almost throughout the year. It is more of a Hindu institution, but there are many differences between the way East and the West Bengalis cook it. In our house, the fish, usually a carp, is always fried first before being put into the *jhol*. To the Bangals of East Bengal that is as good as throwing the fish into the dustbin. The individual cook who tries this recipe can suit his or her personal preference about frying the fish.

 For **Machher jhol** for four hungry people, it is good to have 500 g (1 lb) of fish. In Bengal the favourites are the rui, the katla, or the mirgel, though any big fish can be made into a *jhol*. In the West, cooks can buy any kind of carp and find an approximation of taste, though the difference between the fresh-water fishes of Bengal and the sea fish common abroad will always be strong. Bengalis also cut fish differently from the filleting in Western fish cooking. Once the head and the tail together with the last 10–12 cm (4–5 in) of the body are removed and set aside, the cook decides which portion of the body will be used for the *jhol*. The body of the fish is cut lengthwise, the front or stomach portion being called the *peti* and the back being called the *daga*. The *peti* is preferred for almost any dish since it is oilier and tastier, but the bony *daga* is ideal for the medium of the *jhol*. Whatever the portion chosen, it is then cut horizontally into pieces 2–2.5 cm (¾–1 in) in thickness. Since most families are unable to buy a whole fish, it is common in Bengali markets for the fishmonger to portion his fish and to cut it to the specifications of the client. The fish is rinsed carefully to get rid of all traces of blood and slime, dusted with salt and turmeric and slowly fried in hot oil, two or three pieces at a time. The oil should be heated well before the fish is put in. The salt and turmeric are used not only to reduce the fishy odour but also because they prevent the fish from crumbling or disintegrating, and this makes them almost inevitable ingredients for frying fish, prawn or crabs. Since the skin is left on the fish and tends to sputter in the oil, it is wise to keep your pan covered. Once the fish pieces have been lightly browned, they are lifted out and set aside to drain off all excess oil. If the frying oil has turned too dark, it has to be discarded.

Since two of the several vegetables we commonly use in *jhols* – *patols* and green bananas – may not be available everywhere, I'll stick to the certainties of potatoes and aubergines. Take 4 medium potatoes, peel and cut them into long, flat, 1.25 cm (½ in) thick slices. A medium aubergine should also be cut into matching slices. If *boris* made of dried *dal* paste are available, then 10–12 *kalai dal boris*, white in colour like the *dal* they are made with, are a must for this *jhol*. Apart from these, you need 1 teaspoon of turmeric powder, 2 teaspoons of ground ginger, 1 teaspoon each of ground chilli, cumin and coriander, 1 teaspoon of *panch phoron*, 5–6 green chillies and 2 tablespoons of chopped coriander leaves. The *boris* have to be fried first in 3 tablespoons of heated oil. When they turn brown, lift them out by drawing them up along the sides of the *karai* so that all the oil drains back. The potato slices should also be lightly browned in the same oil and set aside. Then fry the *panch phoron*, add the ground spices, stir for a couple of minutes, add the aubergines and potatoes and pour 900 ml (1½ pints) of water into the *karai*. When it comes to the boil, add the pieces of fried fish, the *boris*, the green chillies and a little salt. The amount of salt has to be carefully judged because there is already salt in the fried fish. As the *jhol* keeps cooking, you can taste and adjust the salt. The whole thing should be kept on the stove until the fish and potatoes are tender – about five to six minutes. Finally, the coriander leaves should be stirred in and the *jhol* removed from the heat. The gravy should be thin and fragrant, but as I said, how thin or how spicy it is depends a lot on personal preference.

A typical Bengali lunch menu in the long hot days of the summer could have a bitter *shukto* or *neembegun* to start with, then a vegetable dish containing at least one of the specially cooling vegetables, followed by the *machher jhol* and perhaps a chutney or sour *ambal* to finish with. The *dal* will figure either after the *shukto* or before the chutney, depending again on individual eating habits.

The three cooling vegetables, *patol*, *jhinge* and *lau*, all belong to the gourd family and are indigenous to Bengal, having a pre-Aryan history. Marrow or courgette could be used as substitutes for them in the West, though the final product will fall far short of the real thing. The *lau*, or white gourd, is now becoming available in many Chinese vegetable shops. Its versatility is most apparent in its combination with evaporated milk, ghee and sugar to make a dessert, a speciality of East Bengal. But my own favourites are *lau-chingri*, with shrimp, and *lau-ghanto*, with coconut, green peas (or brown chick-peas) and crushed *boris*. The former is a Bengali classic. In one of many stories about Gopal Bhar, court jester to Maharaja Krishnachandra of Nabadwip, he slips some shrimp into his tight-fisted widowed aunt's dish of *lau* and, threatening to tell the neighbours that she has been breaking the widows' code of vegetarianism, manages to extract some money from her.

In **Lau-chingri** the gourd's thick green peel is not used, but is preserved to be chopped and fried later as a side dish. For four people to have their fill, we take 750 g (1½ lbs) of young, tender *lau*. Chop it (or any substitute like marrow) into fine narrow pieces about 2.5 cm (1 in) long, throwing out all the seeds. Steam it lightly with a touch of salt and 2 tablespoons of water. If you keep it covered over a low flame, the vegetable will release its own moisture and become very soft. (If it is a very young *lau*, then it does not even need to be steamed.) Set aside the steamed *lau* after draining off any excess moisture and add small *chingri*, shrimp, to this – say, about 250 g (½ lb). The shrimp, peeled and deveined, is dusted with salt and turmeric and fried lightly in oil. Two 2.5 cm (1 in) pieces of cinnamon, 3 cloves and 4 cardamoms are ground for *garom mashla*. You also need 2 teaspoons each of freshly ground cumin and coriander, 1 teaspoon each of chilli and turmeric powder, 3–4 green chillies, salt and sugar to taste and 2–3 teaspoons of ghee.

The *lau*, being watery, requires very little oil, so I heat about 2½ tablespoons in a large *karai*, throw in 2 bay leaves and add the steamed *lau*. After stirring this around for a couple of minutes, I add the shrimp and all the ground spices except the *garom mashla*. The whole thing is then stirred and stirred until all the spices are blended and release their fragrance. Sometimes I sprinkle a little water over the *lau* as I go along, if I notice any tendency for it to stick to the pot. Then I add salt, sugar and green chillies and keep it covered over a low heat for three to four minutes. The sugar should be perceptible, so it is best to start with 3 teaspoons and then to add more if needed. Finally, I uncover the *karai*, stir in the ghee mixed with a pinch of flour and the *garom mashla*, and remove the *lau* from the stove.

For those who are vegetarians and therefore forbidden shrimps, the *lau-ghanto* is a delightful alternative. Not that non-vegetarians abstain from eating it — it is a perennial favourite in our house during the heat of the summer, and it has the advantage of being easier to cook.

For **Lau-ghanto**, again, you need 750 g (1½ lbs) of *lau* (or any gourd substitute), peeled, chopped fine and steamed. All excess water should be pressed out. Grind enough coconut to make 4 tablespoons. Apart from this you need 120 g (4 oz) of green peas, 8–10 *boris* made of *matar dal* (*kalai dal* ones will do at a pinch), 2 teaspoons of ground cumin, 2 bay leaves, 2–3 dry red chillies, salt, sugar, oil, ghee and a little flour. First, the *boris* have to be fried in 2½ tablespoons of hot oil. They should be set aside and a *phoron* of red chillies, bay leaves and whole cumin should be added to the same oil. When they have darkened and the cumin stopped sputtering, I add the steamed *lau*, the peas, the ground coconut and cumin. All this is stirred thoroughly for four to five minutes. Then salt and sugar are added to taste and the *boris* crumbled and mixed into the vegetables. Once the *lau* is quite dry and the peas are tender, I add 2 teaspoons of flour and 2 teaspoons of ghee, mix them well into the vegetables, taste for salt and sugar and remove from the stove. Orthodox Bengali cooks will of course raise their eyebrows at peas and *boris* figuring together, but I quite like breaking conventions if it means variation and improvement in taste.

The second great summer vegetable, *patol*, tends to drive most Bengalis into ecstasy. The eyes of a beautiful Bengali woman are often compared to halved *patols*. A small oval gourd, some 10–15 cm (4–6 in) long, fat in the middle and tapering at both ends, with dark green peel striped longitudinally in a lighter shade of green and creamy firm flesh inside, it is much firmer and less watery than the *lau*. The riper the *patol*, the harder its seeds, something the true aficionado loves. Excellent fried unpeeled as an accompaniment to rice and *dal*, or peeled and cut into pieces in *jhols* and *chachcharis* or even rich *dalnas*, or left whole with the seeds and part of the flesh taken out through a hole at one end and a stuffing of fish or meat put inside to make a *dolma*, the *patol* is essential summer eating. And in this the Bengali has the unequivocal support of Ayurvedic theory, which finds the *patol* to be light and digestive, a curative for worms, fevers, coughs, wind and bile, as well as pleasing to the mind. I have seen canned *patol* (labelled *parwal*, the Hindi term) for sale in some Indian grocery shops in the UK and the US. Though their taste will be nothing like that of the fresh vegetable, they are the only substitutes for the following recipe, since other gourd-like vegetables in the West are much too watery for an approximation of taste and texture.

For **Doi-patol** (or *patol* in yoghurt sauce) for four people, you need 500 g (1 lb) of tender young *patol*. You will also need 120 g (4 oz) of yoghurt, 3 teaspoons of ground ginger, ½ teaspoon each of chilli and turmeric powder, 2 bay leaves, 1 teaspoon of whole cumin seeds, salt and sugar to taste, a tiny pinch of asafoetida, 1 tablespoon of ghee, oil and *garom mashla* ground from 4 cardamoms and 4 pieces of cinnamon, 2.5 cm (1 in) long. No cloves. These *patols*, being young (as will the canned ones), need to be peeled lightly, but they can be left whole with 1.25 cm (½ in) slits being made at both ends. Rinse them in running water and drain. Heat 2½ tablespoons of oil in a *karai* and lightly brown the *patols*. Remove and set aside. The oil will have turned black and so will have to be discarded. Heat another 1½ tablespoons of oil in the *karai*, add 1 tablespoon of ghee to it and throw in a *phoron* of bay leaves, whole cumin seeds and asafoetida. After a minute or so add the ginger-chilli-turmeric and a little salt. Fry the spices well, whip the yoghurt and pour it in. Add the *patols*, some sugar and sprinkle a little water over the whole thing. Cook uncovered for five to six minutes and taste. You can add more salt and sugar if needed. Finally, combine the ghee and *garom mashla*, add to the *patols*, stir once or twice and remove from the stove. Keep covered until serving time.

As spring moves on and the month of Falgun is followed by Chaitra (in mid-March), the midday temperatures become quite taxing. In villages the small ponds and canals start to dry up, but the water shortage is not yet acute and village children enjoy catching all kinds of small fish. On one such hot, dry, cloudless afternoon in late Chaitra, my grand-mother told me the fable about the *chatak* bird, a strange swallow-like creature doomed only to drink rainwater. As the hot, dry weeks progress towards the height of summer, these poor creatures desperately circle the sky looking for the slightest trace of cloud that will bring them life-saving water; in years of excessive heat, their suffering is unbearable.

Popular belief goes that if you refuse to give water to a thirsty person, you will become a *chatak* bird in your next incarnation. Mythical though the story was, it made a great impression on my mind as I pictured to myself the bird's waterless vigil of the skies.

In rural Bengal, and even in certain urban areas, the last day of Chaitra sees the festival of Charak. The religious part of it is mostly observed by wandering *sadhus*, holy men who belong to the Shaiva (devotees of the god Shiva) sect. Having spent part of the month observing fasts and special rituals, they choose this day for masochistic performances in the hope of pleasing Shiva the destroyer, the third of the Hindu trinity. In the old days they would pierce their cheeks and tongues with large iron hooks, claiming to feel no pain. Iron rods which pierced the skin of their backs would be attached to a tall wooden contraption that would whirl them round and round until they fell to the ground unconscious and bleeding. Many of them died of tetanus and other infections. Thankfully, the government banned the use of iron hooks and rods in 1863, but lesser acts of self-torture are still performed in front of gawking audiences at the Charak fairs.

With the month of Baisakh the dry heat of summer is at its highest, to be followed by the oppressive humidity which will be relieved by the monsoon. A folk rhyme listing all the rituals that Bengali Hindus should perform through the months of the year describes the watering of *tulsi* plants (wild basil, sacred to Krishna) as the appropriate one for Baisakh. In spite of this parching heat, Baisakh is a great time for Hindu weddings. The Hindu almanacs, based on ancient scriptural calculations, have designated several months of the year as *malomash*, inauspicious for weddings. So all weddings are scheduled during the other permissible months on the specific auspicious days marked in the calendar. The final month of the year, Chaitra, is a *malomash* and with the beginning of the new year the mood is all set for the festivity of weddings. For some reason, the first month of the year has extra auspicious connotations.

When my mother and father were married in the early 1940s, wedding feasts still followed tradition. Banana leaves were spread in front of each guest; once the meal was eaten, the leaves would be thrown away and a new set of leaves placed before the next batch of guests, thus saving on washing up and forestalling the dangers of inadequate cleaning. First there would be *luchis*, thin golden discs of rolled out dough fried in ghee, to be eaten with fried greens and some other fried vegetable like *patol* or aubergine. Next would come the famous Bengali *chhanchra*, mixed vegetables cooked with the entrails and oil of fish, followed by a rich *dal*. Once all of this had been mopped up with innumerable *luchis*, a lovely rui fish made into a rich *kalia* redolent of *garom mashla* would be served with *polao*.

This *polao* was no approximation or base imitation, as is so common today. Only the best quality rice, Basmati or some other fragrant variety, would be used. The huge quantities of ghee required to make *polao* for 300 or 400 people would also be absolutely pure, unadulterated with vegetable shortening. The water in which the rice would be cooked was called the *akhni* water, that is water in which whole *garom mashla* as well as other expensive spices like mace, nutmeg, saffron, *sajira* (a kind of cumin) and a handful of yellow split peas had been boiled for a long time – the usual duration was the time needed to reduce the original water to one-third of its volume. This incredibly fragrant water – once the spice bundle, like a bouquet garni, was discarded – would then be added to the rice fried in ghee, and the *polao* that was produced was a delight all by itself. Sadly, the fabulous prices of good ghee, fine rice and the ingredients for *akhni* water have made that *polao* a dream from the past. The 'fried rice' or 'vegetable *polao*' served at most weddings today is made with ordinary rice and cooked in peanut oil with a few chopped vegetables thrown in.

In very wealthy houses in those days, the rui *kalia* was often accompanied by another fish preparation, of either king prawn or hilsa, but meat was usually not part of a Hindu

wedding feast. For the vegetarians there would be an extra
item of curried *channa* or *dhonkas* made of ground *dal*. After
the fish came a chutney (tomatoes, green mangoes, green
papayas, dried plums, according to season and taste) served
with crisp *papor* (*papadam* in other parts of India). Last, but
not least, came the sweet yoghurt, *mishti doi*, with a variety
of sweets and, as a final chaser, the sweet-spiced *paan*.

The average wedding menu today, especially in a city like
Calcutta, hardly bears any resemblance to this menu of the
1940s. As meat became more and more acceptable, even in
the most orthodox houses, it became the fashion to serve a
meat *kalia* after the fish, and, by the 1960s, when I was old
enough to go to weddings or observe the food at weddings in
my own family, all the initial items of fried greens, *chhanchra*
and *dal* were being dropped because they were troublesome.
Later even the *kalia* made with rui fish disappeared: in its
place the non-vegetarian guests were given fillets of bhetki,
coated with egg and breadcrumbs and deep-fried in oil, or a
fish 'chop' followed by a meat *kalia*.

Today's weddings have slipped even further. They often
take place at houses hired for the occasion, the food is
supplied by catering companies which bring the pre-cooked
food which they re-heat and serve on china plates. No longer
for us the pleasure of touching the shining green of banana
leaves, nor the excitement of the preparations. Each wedding
in our house during my childhood carries memories of hectic
activities in one corner of the huge roof, where the
professional cooks would set up their wood and coal stoves
and be busy cooking all day. Even a couple of days before the
wedding the house was full of relatives working away. Then
would come the arrival of Anath uncle, the wholesale
fishmonger whom my uncle had befriended, sitting in the
courtyard in front of a huge *ansh-bonti*, dismembering one
huge rui after another, the blood and entrails of the fish
spilling all around him. And apart from the *mishti doi*,
ordered from one of the famous Calcutta sweet shops, the
other sweets were all made at home by hired cooks who never

minded when I slipped upstairs and stood watching their
activities, and inevitably grinned when I reached out a greedy
little paw for a surreptitious handful. I will never forget the
fresh taste and fragrance of those sweets, still hot from the
huge *karai*. Nothing tasted half as good when bought from
the shops. Munching the sweets, I would wander over to the
other cooks who were boiling the *akhni* water for the *polao*
and take a few heady breaths before trotting demurely
downstairs, my mouth and hands wiped clean of all sticky
traces.

The Bangladesh wedding feast is quite another matter. The
Muslim élite's fondness for meat has set the standards for the
middle class too, and the wedding menu probably has
remained constant for the last half-century. The very first
wedding I attended in Dhaka was that of a friend of my
husband's. At the wedding feast the menu was simple, and I
was to see it repeated, with minor variations, at all subsequent
weddings during my seven years in Dhaka. Instead of plain
polao, there was a *biryani*, rice cooked with meat. There were
round brown *shami kebabs* and there was a *jhal gosht* made
with beef. A yoghurt and cucumber *raita* and a dessert of *firni*
completed the meal. All of these items are to be seen all over
northern India and in Indian restaurants abroad.

The similarity of the Bangladeshi wedding menu tends to
pall – 'Yet another wedding invitation!' is a genuine
expression of gustatory boredom – but in the hands of the
gifted cook each of these items takes on the attributes of a
classic. Of the many possible combinations of rice and meat,
probably the tastiest is the *kachchi biryani* made with rice
and *khashi* meat. Bangladeshi Muslims seem to have an
exclusive preference for *khashi* or castrated goat meat over
ordinary goat meat. Over the years the Hindus too have
learnt to eat the rich, fatty *khashi* meat (in Calcutta mostly
Muslim butchers sell it), but they also enjoy the special taste
of the tender flesh of the kid goat. In Bangladesh this is
almost unknown. Even chicken is made into capons by
Muslims, especially in Dhaka, Noakhali and Chittagong.

Unlike other rice preparations made with meat and rice, in *kachchi biryani* the meat is uncooked when added to the rice. As a result the dish requires slow cooking over low heat and makes for very tender textured meat. Some people find it too rich to stomach. Others, like my friend Farhad Ghuznavi, whose feudal background is well reflected in his tastes, feel it is the only kind of *biryani* worth having. Just before leaving Dhaka for good, I was fortunate enough to be shown one way of making the *kachchi biryani* by Nilufar, a woman who worked with me. It is never a success if you try to make it in small quantities, nor is it too much effort to make a lot of it, since you can make a complete meal out of it with a salad on the side. The predominant flavour is that of the rich fatty meat transmuted into an unoppressive spiciness by the technique of sealed cooking. Though the process is painstaking, the results are well worth it.

For **Kachchi biryani** for eight people, you need 1 kg (2 lbs) of fine Basmati rice and 2 kg (4 lbs) of *khashi* or lamb. Bony pieces like lamb chops will be better than solid meat like the leg. When I went into the kitchen, Nilufar had already cut the meat into medium-sized pieces, washed it and left it mixed with 2 tablespoons of salt to generate moisture and soften the meat. After half an hour the meat was rinsed and left in a colander to drain. Meanwhile she organised her spices. Two large onions were sliced fine and lightly browned in a little ghee, ginger was ground to make 2 tablespoons and garlic for 1 tablespoon, 6 cardamoms, 6 cloves and 2 pieces of cinnamon, 2.5 cm (1 in) long, were ground to a powder, as was 1 whole nutmeg. By now the fried onions had cooled and she ground them coarsely on the stone – you can crush them in a mortar, too. She then transferred the meat to the large cooking pot and mixed it thoroughly with all these fresh ground spices, adding 1 tablespoon of cumin powder, a large pinch of mace and 3 tablespoons of roasted red chilli powder. After this 300 g (10 oz) of yoghurt and 4 tablespoons of *keora* water were added to the meat.

Leaving the meat to marinate a little, she took about 500 g (1 lb) of medium potatoes, peeled and quartered them and fried them in a little oil. As the potatoes turned golden, she sprinkled some yellow food colouring over them (turmeric would produce an incompatible taste and odour). Originally the recipe calls for saffron, but this is so prohibitively expensive in Bangladesh that most people use food colouring. The fried potatoes were placed over the meat and 120 ml (4 fl oz) of ghee poured over it. Once again, she left the meat to marinate and proceeded to deal with the rice, rinsing it under the tap and then draining it in a colander. She also set 3 l (6 pints) of water and 2 tablespoons of salt to boil in a large pot. As soon as the water boiled the rice was added to it. When it came to a second boil she carefully poured out most of the water into another pan and then left the rice to drain. From the water she took 250 ml (8 fl oz), mixed it with 120 ml (4 fl oz) of ghee and added it to the meat, which was left covered to marinate for half an hour. Meanwhile she set some water to boil in a medium-sized pan.

Finally it was time to cook. She spread the drained half-cooked rice evenly over the meat and potatoes and sprinkled some more yellow food colouring over it. Then she added the last 120 ml (4 fl oz) of ghee and poured some more of the salted hot rice water into the pan so that it was level – not more – with the rice. Covering the pot with a well-fitting lid, she sealed it with a thick flour and water paste, put the saucepan of boiling water on top and finally placed the sealed pot over a high flame. After about twenty minutes she reduced the heat to a very low flame and left it undisturbed for nearly one and a half hours. Later I found you can always cook this *kachchi biryani* by placing it for three hours in an oven heated to 180°C (350°F, gas mark 4). The important thing is to seal the lid to the pot and to have the heat come from above and below. By the time it was done, the entire kitchen was full of the wonderful *biryani* smell. Before serving, Nilufar stirred the contents of the pot so that the rice, potatoes and meat were well mixed. She regretted that she had no almonds or pistachios, otherwise she would have added them to the meat before cooking.

The other favourite served at weddings as well as private dinners is the uniquely Bengali Muslim dish, the *rezala*. This is made with *khashi* meat and, though not overly spicy, tends to linger on the palate. The milk and the saffron in the dish produce a beautifully tinted gravy, while the sharp fragrance of the green chillies combines with other elements to produce a most unforgettable bouquet. No doubt there are minor variations that good cooks bring to their *rezala*, but the one I was taught by my friend's mother seems fairly standard.

 For the eight people she had invited that evening, she had bought 2 kg (4 lbs) of meat, cubed and washed, to make the **Khashir rezala**. This she combined in a large pot with 250 g (8 oz) of grated onion, 2 tablespoons of ground ginger, 3 teaspoons of ground garlic, 5–6 whole cardamoms, 5–6 pieces of cinnamon, 2.5 cm (1 in) long, 250 g (8 oz) of yoghurt, 1 tablespoon of sugar, 3 teaspoons of salt and 250 ml (8 fl oz) of ghee. Once all of this was thoroughly mixed, she covered the pot and let it cook on a low flame for about half an hour. Then she uncovered and stirred the meat well and kept it covered again until all the moisture had evaporated and the ghee was visible. Then she took 250 ml (8 fl oz) of warm whole milk, added a tiny pinch of saffron to it and poured it over the meat. Next, 20 whole green chillies were added, the heat reduced to a minimum and the meat left tightly covered for about half an hour before it was ready to serve. When my sister-in-law made this *rezala*, she always selected fresh, not dried, red and ripened chillies for the dish. They stood out in a most pleasing contrast against the pale yellow of the gravy.

In the advancing heat of Baisakh, such rich preparations become hard to stomach, even for those who can afford them, and the diet of the have-nots, especially in rural Bengal, seems more attractive. Many of them are too poor to eat fish every day and one of the summer staples is *pantabhat*, or fermented rice. Left-over rice, when there is an adequate supply of it, will be covered with water and kept overnight in the kitchen where the heat will ferment it by morning. For the peasant who has a hard day's work ahead of him, it is a substantial breakfast seasoned with hot fried chillies, raw onions or even bits of left-over vegetables. Though my childhood was strictly urban, I was no stranger to the *pantabhat*, for my mother and grandmother both enjoyed it with chillies and sour pickles on hot summer afternoons. Somehow I could never feel enthusiastic about the slightly sour taste of the fermented rice, and avoided it even when offered.

In Bangladesh I learned how delightful *pantabhat* can taste when one is ravenously hungry. I was working on a drinking-water survey and had to make several trips to nearby villages. Around the middle of Baisakh three of us went to a village near Munshiganj, a small town in the district of Dhaka. The Buriganga River, attenuated in the heat, and the leaden stillness of the sky made us long for a summer storm, but there were no clouds to promise relief as we trudged along the uneven, dusty village paths. In places the land had cracked open, and obviously irrigation could not be done extensively in the village. By the time we had finished our work, we were both famished and parched. The hand-pump wells in the village gave us cool water, but there was no food in sight. Even the teashops were closed. The village seemed so god-forsaken and the people so poor and emaciated that we did not have the heart to ask for any food, but their own permanent deprivations had made them sensitive to others' needs. After much whispering, an old man stepped forward and asked us to come to his cottage for something to eat. He would not take no for an answer and so, under his badly thatched roof, we sat cross-legged on a torn mat and ate *pantabhat* with some very hot vegetable dish to which a few shrimps had been added. The kindness and sincere hospitality of that man whom I never saw again were seasonings that made our meal taste better than any wedding feast of *biryani*. Today the taste still comes back to me like cool shade on a very hot day.

The heat of Baisakh is turned to productive uses by the women of Bengal. The third day after the new moon of Baisakh, *Akshaytritya*, is the appointed day for both Hindus and Muslims to make *kasundi*, our version of table mustard. Bengali mustard seed is dark and pungent and is a favourite ingredient, ground with green chillies, in making dishes with certain fishes and vegetables. *Kasundi* is a kind of mustard pickle in which the ground mustard is combined with green mangoes or tamarind or lemon (to provide a sour taste) as well as with oil and other spices. Most Bengali pickles are made by drying in the sun, instead of being cooked or preserved in vinegar. Baisakh, therefore, is an ideal time to start. Women are particularly enthusiastic about this domestic activity. The love of sourness seems almost genetically coded into young Bengali girls, and just as children in the West hanker for sweets, Bengali girls will do anything to pick all kinds of sour fruit or steal sour pickles from their mother's larder.

Making a good *kasundi* was considered even more difficult than making good pickles and women tended to guard their recipes jealously. It is now a lost art in the cities where commercially bottled *kasundi* is widely sold, but village women still make it, purifying themselves first, as for all other things that have to be preserved through the year. Some families resolutely refuse to make *kasundi* because they believe that if they do so a member of their family is sure to die. In my own family another very restrictive superstition still holds sway: all pickles, *kasundi* and *boris* are inauspicious for travel. Despite the innumerable trips I have made from Calcutta, I have never succeeded in carrying any of these with me.

While the pickles are preserved in the sun, human beings find even the slightest effort exhausting. Rain is badly needed by way of relief, and if Baisakh does not have its rainstorms, land and life are both endangered. As Sharatchandra Chattop-adhyay writes in *Mahesh*:

It was almost the end of Baisakh, but not even the shadow
of a cloud was visible. Fire seemed to rain down from the
sky. The huge field stretching all the way to the horizon
had been baked and burnt under the sun until it had
cracked all over, and from these countless crevices the
earth's blood seemed to dissipate endlessly into smoke.
Staring too long at its reptilian upward motion made your
head swim – almost like some powerful intoxicant.

Mahesh, the protagonist of this story, is a bullock owned by a
poor Muslim peasant, Ghafur. During a terrible drought
Ghafur finds himself unable not only to pay his dues to the
landlord but also to provide for himself, his daughter and
even his beloved Mahesh. Driven by hunger, Mahesh
encroaches on the landlord's sacrosanct pastureland, for
which he is duly punished by the landlord's henchmen.
Finally the dumb beast, deprived even of water to slake his
thirst, dies before his helpless master's eyes. Ghafur, stripped
of whatever little he owned, like so many landless peasants
before and after him, leaves his ancestral village forever with
his daughter, his only prayer to Allah being that those who
deprived Mahesh of god-given grass and water should receive
their proper punishment.

But there are other years when Baisakh is kind and, though
the pickle-makers may curse, the earth celebrates the
appearance of short violent rainstorms, *kalbaisakhis*, that
bring the temperatures down dramatically and leave the
dehydrated earth replenished, the trees washed, the air free of
dust. Destructive though they can be, flattening fruit and
standing crops, the first onrush of dark clouds, like an
irresistible army in the north-western sky, only arouses
feelings of joy in the beholder.

One afternoon in Dhaka when I was coming back to my
house in Dhanmondi from a friend's in Tejgaon, I was caught
in a *kalbaisakhi*. It had been an oppressive afternoon and as I
got into the rickshaw I could see a familiar darkening of one
corner of the horizon. Foolishly, I thought the wheel of the

rickshaw could beat the demons of the sky, but a drenching
in the rain was not going to be the end of the story, for soon a
storm of hailstones started falling. The driver abandoned me
on the deserted road, ran across the pavement and stood
under a tree while I sat trapped in the rickshaw, resigned but
not afraid, until the dark grey road, brick-and-cement
pavement and bits of grass were magically transformed into a
white expanse of cobbled ice.

The last and most terrible month of summer, Jaishtha,
from mid-May to mid-June, is a boon for fruit lovers.
Ripening mangoes and jackfruits, white translucent kernels
of the unripe palm, sweet and tangy lychees, vivid and juicy
watermelon, bland *jamrul* and even astringent *kalojam*
abound in the markets. The different varieties of mangoes –
West Bengal's *himsagar*, Benares's *langra*, *chousa* and *dusseri*
from Uttar Pradesh – are served as snacks and desserts, for
breakfast and for *jalkhabar*, our version of afternoon tea.
And sometimes we have the rich delight of mango pulp mixed
into *kheer*, thick, rich evaporated milk.

The heat also prompts frequent servings of yoghurt or milk
mixed with *chira* (flattened rice soaked in water) and
mangoes or bananas, called *phalahar*. This was most in
evidence in our house every Tuesday in Jaishtha, when
women other than widows had to observe the ritual of
Jaimangalbar. More a folk custom than a strictly religious
occasion, the purpose was to appease the goddess
Mangalchandi and gain her protection for the family. All fish,
meat, onions and garlic were forbidden. At lunch the
phalahar would be served and in the evening we would have
luchis with vegetables. Another observance in Jaishtha, once
common among rural Hindu women in Bengal, was the
Sabitribrata, on the day before the Jaishtha new moon. The
women would fast all day without touching a drop of water
in that dreadful heat. In the evening, after breaking fast, they
would have to feed a Brahmin – all this in the hope of
avoiding the pain of widowhood.

Obviously there is nothing like faith to take the mind off

hunger and thirst. In Bangladesh the month of Ramzan in the Islamic calendar happened to fall in Jaishtha one year when I was there. I was amazed at the will and cheerful endurance of those who fasted, especially while doing a whole day's work at the office. In the evening, after saying the *maghreb* (evening) prayers, they would enjoy their light meal of *iftaar*, which always began with a cool drink – lemonade, green coconut water, or even the juice and pulp of watermelon. Though I did not fast, I always enjoyed watching the *iftaar* being brought in: soaked *chira* with ground coconut and sugar, brown local chick-peas fried with one or two red chillies, mango slices and flat discs of fried ground lentils seasoned with green chilli and onion. By contrast, when Ramzan was over and the great festival of Id-ul-fitr arrived, I was overwhelmed and almost oppressed by the weight of the rich food.

After occasional bouts of heavy meals like these in Dhaka during the summer, I used to long for my mother's light touch and some of the bland, cool summer items from my childhood. My first year in Dhaka was spent searching fruitlessly for *posto*, the tiny white poppy seeds from which all opium has been extracted. Apart from being considered easily digestible in the summer heat, *posto* also has a uniquely delicate taste which caresses the palate without arousing it. But the early 1970s were bad times in Bangladesh and many ordinary things were hard to get. Today *posto* is available around the world, so some of the easiest and most delicious recipes can be tried anywhere too.

 The simplest is a **Posto chutney** made by grinding the *posto* together with some coconut, green chillies, a few cloves of garlic and slices of green mango. The paste is seasoned with salt and sugar to taste. In the absence of green mangoes, lemon juice can be used.

Posto bata also requires no cooking and is eaten in small quantities as a starter with rice, almost like a relish. For the three of us my mother usually took 50 g (1.6 oz) of *posto*, soaked it in water for half an hour and ground it fine on the stone. The texture should be tight, not watery. Then she would mix it with some fresh mustard oil, salt and chopped green chillies. All these ingredients can vary in quantity according to taste, and in the absence of a grinding stone a mixer or food processor can be used.

As a variant on this, known as **Posto batar chachchari**, she would sometimes take 100 g (3½ oz) of ground *posto*, heat 1 tablespoon of oil and 1 tablespoon of ghee in her *karai*, throw in 1 finely chopped medium onion, fry it brown, add the *posto* with 1 teaspoon of ground cumin, ½ teaspoon of chilli powder, salt and a little sugar. All these would be stirred with a little water being sprinkled over the mixture from time to time to avoid burning. When the *posto* was nicely browned, she would add 1 teaspoon of ghee mixed with some ground *garom mashla* (2 cardamoms, 2 pieces of cinnamon, no cloves).

For **Alu posto**, take 250 g (½ lb) potatoes and peel, cube and fry them light brown in 2½ tablespoons of oil. Set aside and fry in the same oil 1 finely chopped large onion. When this turns brown add the potatoes, some salt, 4-5 green chillies and 250 ml (8 fl oz) of water. Keep covered over a medium heat until the potatoes are tender. Add 100 g (3 oz) of finely ground *posto* and stir over high heat until all water has evaporated.

You can also make a more substantial dish with *posto*. By the time I had located the seeds in the Dhaka market, I had already tasted two Bangladeshi preparations using *posto*. As is only to be expected from the Muslims, they were *khashi* and chicken, not vegetables, and they were delicious. The chicken was made by the wife of the friend whose wedding had provided me with my first intimate look at a Bangladeshi Muslim marriage. She was a quiet, shy girl who appeared to be totally dominated by her headstrong husband until I saw her walk out on him with her month-old baby because she felt her parents had been insulted. They were reconciled later, and no doubt their daily life was sweetened by her wonderful talents as a cook.

 For **Chicken with posto** for eight people she had taken two plump medium-sized chickens. Skinned, portioned into 10–12 pieces each and washed, the birds were combined in a large pot with 250 g (8 oz) of yoghurt, 250 g (8 oz) of grated onion, 1 tablespoon of ground ginger, 1 teaspoon each of ground garlic and coriander, 2 teaspoons of ground cumin, 1 tablespoon of chilli powder, 2 tablespoons of ground *posto*, 1 teaspoon of ground fennel, ½ teaspoon of ground mace, 60 g (2 oz) of almonds, blanched and slivered, 60 g (2 oz) of raisins, 2 tablespoons of salt and 120 ml (4 fl oz) of peanut oil and 120 ml (4 fl oz) of ghee. The whole thing, well mixed, was cooked, tightly covered, on a very low heat for an hour. Then she checked to see if the flesh was tender. You can add extra water if you find the chicken tough and stringy. Once it is done, the meat is stirred over a high heat until it is nicely coated in the oil/ghee and spices, with no moisture left. Before serving you can sprinkle some extra almonds on top. A *polao*, instead of plain boiled rice, is a good accompaniment.

As for the other preparation, I discovered it not in Dhaka but in the town of Rajshahi, in the northern Bangladesh district of the same name. To most Bengalis Rajshahi is famous for two things: the best *langra* mangoes outside Benares and the wonderful *kanchagolla*, a kind of milk-based sweet, made in Natore on the outskirts of the city. For me, however, the trip had more romantic associations. During my girlhood one of the most famous Bengali poems we read was about the fabled heroine of Natore, Banalata Sen, she whose eyes promised all the warmth and sanctuary a fledgeling finds in its nest. Wandering around the ancient royal palace of Natore, near Rajshahi, I was told by one of my guides that the deserted areas all around were prime land for the cultivation of poppy and marijuana. On the three evenings I spent in that realm of poetic fancy and poppy seeds, my host's cook produced the most unforgettable dinners. He served this *khashi* and *posto* creation on the last night of my visit. Since *khashi* is not available in the West, good spring lamb can be substituted. It must not be too fatty, for the odour of the fat will destroy the delicate flavour. Lamb chops are the best portion to choose, though they entail a lot of work in the careful excision of morsels of fat.

 For **Lamb with posto** for four people, take 1 kg (2 lbs) of lamb, cut it into small pieces (keeping the bones in), rinse it in water and set aside. Chop 2 large onions, a 5 cm (2 in) long piece of ginger and an entire small head of garlic as finely as possible. In a thick-bottomed pot melt 60 g (4 oz) of unsalted butter or heat 120 g (4 oz) of ghee over a medium flame. Add 4–5 sticks of cinnamon, 6 whole cardamoms and 4 bay leaves. When these have been fried for a couple of minutes, add the chopped onion, ginger and garlic and fry them until brown. Add the meat, 2 teaspoons of salt and 3 teaspoons of sugar, and keep stirring over a medium heat. As the meat is being browned, put 60 g (2 oz) of *posto* in a bowl, cover it with hot water and set aside. Keep stirring the meat until it is very dark and starts sticking to the pot. Add 6–7 whole dry red chillies and the *posto* and water. Add some more hot water, enough to cover the meat, cover the pot tightly and leave on a low flame till the meat is absolutely tender. Uncover and taste for salt and sugar balance, adding whatever is necessary. The sweetness should be somewhat pronounced. Finish over a high flame. All water should evaporate and the meat should be coated with the butter/ghee and spices. Though no ground spices are used, the chillies provide sharpness of taste and the minute graininess of the *posto* counters the tenderness of the meat very well. Sometimes I have tried using green chillies instead of dried red ones, and this gives a different piquancy to the dish.

Among the Hindus of West Bengal, the most memorable domestic ritual in Jaishtha is Jamaishashthi, on the sixth day after the new moon. There are many *shashthis*, sixth days of the moon, through the Bengali year which the Hindus have loaded with significance, all of them for the benefit of their children. On this one, sons-in-law are blessed by the parents-in-law, given gifts and ceremoniously fed a huge meal, obviously a relic of the times when women were totally dependent on their husbands and the parents would do their best to appease the mortal god who held the happiness of their daughter in his hands. When I was a child my grandmother would give new clothes to all her sons-in-law, including my father, and there would be a general bustle leading to the special meal. Though tradition demanded a whole head of rui fish for each son-in-law, I do not think we were so particular.

Years later, I was quite amazed at the care my mother took to please my Muslim husband when she entertained him for Jamaishashthi. There was no traditional fish head, for she knew he could not stomach it. But apart from the obligatory *dal* and fried vegetables, there was a wonderful dish made with green jackfruit whose firm flesh has given it the nickname 'tree-goat' in Bengali. It was one of his favourite vegetables and my mother had managed to find that out. On that hot stifling day, there was no meat, but a variety of carefully selected fish preparations instead. The first to be served was a peculiar specimen called the topshe or tapaswi, a small fish about 20 cm (8½ in) long, which is served whole, first marinated in onion-ginger paste, then coated with egg and breadcrumbs and deep-fried in oil. Bengalis consider this a delicacy and my husband was very fond of it, the more so because it was a rarity in the Dhaka markets. The name tapaswi means one who meditates, and is supposed to have arisen from the ample whiskers, like those of a holy man, sported by the fish. The British called it the mango fish, perhaps because the season for the two coincide. One Englishman is supposed to have said that all his financial losses and his mental and physical sufferings in India were amply compensated by his good fortune in having tasted the mango fish of Bengal. Those my mother served that day were plump with roe.

After the topshe came rui in yoghurt sauce, followed by fishballs made out of a bony fish called chitol. My mother learnt to make the fishballs from one of her Bangal colleagues, and I must say that they were a great success. We call them *koptas* or *baras*, but they are also given the charming name of *muithya* – something made in the *muthi* or fist – by some East Bengal people. I think both recipes are likely to be appreciated everywhere. Usefully, they can be duplicated with whatever large fish is available.

To prepare **Doi machh** (or fish with yoghurt): if you have 500 g (1 lb) of fish (we like the carp varieties for this), cut them horizontally into long 2.5 cm (1 in) thick pieces. The *peti* or frontal stomach portion is specially suitable for this. Wash the fish, dust it with a little salt and turmeric and fry it lightly in oil. Remove and set aside to drain off all excess oil. Meanwhile whip 250 g (8 oz) of yoghurt and mix 1 tablespoon of sugar in with it. Chop 3 medium onions very fine and grind enough ginger to give you 1 tablespoon. In a *karai* heat 4–5 tablespoons of oil, add 1 teaspoon of ghee, and throw in whole *garom mashla* (3 sticks of cinnamon, 4 cloves, 4 cardamoms) and 2 bay leaves. After a minute, add the onion and ginger with 1 teaspoon of turmeric. Fry these until brown, add the yoghurt and a little salt. As soon as it comes to boil, add the fish and 5–6 green chillies, reduce the heat to low and keep covered for six to eight minutes. Uncover, check for salt and sugar balance and remove. If you wish, you can garnish this, as the Bangals would, with chopped coriander leaves.

For **Chitol kopta** (or fishballs in sauce) for four people, 500 g (1 lb) of fish will be enough. In Bengal the flesh is scooped away from the skin of the bony back portion with a spoon, but you have to be careful to move the spoon the way the bones are laid. If it moves against them, the bones will come away with the fish. To make the fishballs, first boil and finely mash 2 medium potatoes. Mix these very thoroughly with the lump of fish. Though chitol, being very sticky, does not need this as a binder, I find the potatoes make the texture soft and fluffy. To the fish and potato mixture add some salt, ½ teaspoon of ground ginger, 1 medium onion chopped very fine and 1 beaten egg. Mix all of these together to make a tight dough-like lump. It should not be thin or watery. Divide it into 20 round or oval balls, patting each smooth between the palms. Then heat some oil, say 120 ml (4 fl oz), in a *karai* and deep-fry the fishballs in it. In the hot oil they will swell up like little balloons, though they shrink later when taken out. These *koptas* can be served by themselves as an appetiser or snack, or just as an item with rice and *dal*.

But mostly they are put into a thick sauce before serving with rice. For this, you need 2 finely chopped medium onions, ½ teaspoon of ground ginger, 1 teaspoon of chilli powder, ½ teaspoon of turmeric powder, salt, sugar, 2 bay leaves and whole *garom mashla* (3 pieces of cinnamon, 4 cardamoms, 4 cloves). If the oil in which you have fried the fishballs has been reduced too much, you can add some fresh oil and heat it. Then throw in the bay leaves and *garom mashla*, fry for a couple of minutes, add the onions and fry till golden brown. Add 2 teaspoons of sugar and wait till it turns to a caramel colour, after which add the other spices. Fry these well, add 500 ml (16 fl oz) of water and salt as needed. When it comes to the boil, add the fishballs and keep covered for five to six minutes. Taste for salt, add 2 teaspoons of flour to thicken the sauce and remove. Once again, you can use less or more water, depending on how much sauce you would like, and the spices will have to be adjusted accordingly. This, too, can be garnished with coriander leaves. Or you can mix in a small handful of freshly chopped mint to the fish mixture before making the fishballs.

True to form, my husband was unable to eat anything near as

much as my mother would like. As I watched the battle of wills between mother and son-in-law, I realised how odd poor people would have found this reluctance for food. I remembered a one-time maid who used to sniff and recite a proverb whenever she saw such carryings on among her betters. 'The son-in-law now refuses the delectable head of rui we have given him; but one fine day he'll have to go down on his hands and knees to look for what the rice thresher left behind.' The other side of the coin is the typical Bengali male, who feels affronted unless his wife serves him with every item on the table.

Four days after the adoration of the son-in-law it is Dashahara, the day on which bathing in the Ganga is said to clean one of the ten deadly sins that besmirch mankind. It is also said that if it does not rain on Dashahara, the family of serpents will multiply rapidly to the detriment of human life in the monsoon. Unfortunately there are many Dashaharas when it does not rain. Many whole Jaishthas, in fact, go without rain. The unimaginable suffering of people and animals can only be relieved by the monsoon. In some villages life comes to a standstill; even with irrigation the crops suffer, and anyway, it is mostly rich farmers who have access to irrigation pumps. People, especially women, have to trek miles to find a source of drinking water, since very often the modern hand-pump tubewells are in a state of disrepair. A passage from *Mahesh* gives us a real sense of the killer heat that leaves all creation panting, waiting for the rainclouds of Asharh like the proverbial *chatak* bird:

> Jaishtha was almost over. It was only by confronting the sky today that one could comprehend how much greater the sheer ruthlessness of destructive nature could be than during Baisakh, terrible as that had been. No hint of mercy was to be perceived. It was almost frightening to think that the shape of things could ever change, that this same sky could show itself one day clad in tender, moisture-laden clouds. Rather, it seemed that the fire which rained down

day after day from this ignited sky was infinite, endless — that it would not rest till all was consumed.

But life does go on regenerating itself, and things do change. In time, or unbearably late, the monsoon does come to Bengal, the utter deathly stillness of summer heat broken by the roll of thunder and the onrush of wind and cloud from the Bay of Bengal. Until then, excruciating though it is, land, crops and living creatures expand their beings to the last point of waiting.

Barsha

MONSOON

During the last few days of summer, each longer than the previous one, the endurance of man, land, animals and vegetation is stretched to breaking point. As the people of Bengal live through this scorching, humid hell, waiting for Barsha, the monsoon, some find comfort in quoting the opening phrase of the *Meghadootam*, a Sanskrit love poem by the Indian poet Kalidasa, '*Asharasya prathama dibase*' –

'On the first day of Asharh' – for this is the month which will bring the relief of rain, gentle and violent, to an exhausted earth.

Nature, of course, does not always conform to calendar dates. Though the first of the mystic month of Asharh falls in the middle of June, Barsha is sometimes delayed by as much as two or three weeks. In some years there is the welcome presage of a short but violent pre-monsoon downpour, after which the silent summer oppression returns with renewed force for many more days. When the monsoon does finally set in, it too is the most deceptive advent, arriving with sweet succour from the parching heat and showing nothing of the fury which will later swell the rivers to cause ruinous floods.

But then who can think of future disaster while enjoying the immediate relief of life-giving showers? As children, even the first sight of dark clouds rolling towards us from the distant south-east would set us skipping with excitement. The anticipation intensified as the winds gathered force, as the low rumble of thunder was heard and the first streaks of lightning rent the sky. It is hard to remain unresponsive to what Rabindranath Tagore called the 'terrible rapture' of the oncoming monsoon. As the first drops fell, we would rush clamorously out onto the streets or up on the roof for a ritual drenching.

The first day of Barsha is generally honoured with the eating of a special meal, made more enjoyable by the drastic drop in temperature created by the rains and cloud-covered sky. The best known Bengali dish associated with the monsoon is *khichuri*, rice and *dal* cooked together with certain spices. This is the housewife's response to the sudden arrival of the monsoon rains, or heavy rain at any other time of the year. Though simple, it is a superb dish which requires care and does not survive neglect or inattention. It is probably one of the oldest surviving dishes in the Bengali repertoire. From wandering mendicants who begged for their food to various religious orders that observed a strict simplicity of diet, countless people have depended on *khichuri* to give them a balanced meal. Without any trimmings, it can be even rice and *dal* boiled together in a pot. Slum dwellers in Indian cities can still be seen making *khichuris* on the pavements. With the refinements of certain spices, it becomes a delicacy which is not too rich for frequent consumption. After 200 years of colonial rule, the British also took it home with them as kedgeree. Like 'curry', kedgeree probably was a contribution of the Indian (often Muslim) chef working in the British officer's home. The simplest form of *khichuri* was probably a welcome addition to the heavily-laden breakfast table, a departure from the usual porridge.

There are of course many kinds of *khichuris*, depending on what kind of *dal* is being used. The consistency may be thin, thick, or dry and fluffy like a pilaf, plain or with seasonal winter vegetables like new potatoes, green peas and cauliflower added to the basic rice-*dal* mixture. The one constant factor is the use of *atap* rice, usually of the short-grained variety. The other characteristic of *khichuri* is that, whatever the consistency, each grain of rice and *dal* has to be fully cooked but not soft enough to lose its identity. This is why, although it is quick and easy to make, it needs careful watching. As the rice and *dal* are cooked and the water reduces, the *khichuri* tends to stick to the pot and can easily burn.

 One of my favourite recipes for **Simple khichuri** requires, for five people, 500 g (1 lb) of *atap* rice (Basmati, available in the West, can be used since short-grained varieties are not available) and 500 g (1 lb) of roasted *moong dal*. For seasoning I use *garom mashla* of 4 sticks of cinnamon, 2.5 cm (1 in) long, 4–5 whole cardamoms and 4–5 whole cloves; a liberal pinch of whole cumin seeds; 2 bay leaves; a finely-chopped piece of ginger 4 cm (1½ in) long; 2 whole green chillies; 1½ teaspoons of turmeric powder; 60 ml (2 fl oz) of mustard or any other cooking oil like corn or peanut oil; salt and sugar to taste and ghee.

The rice and *dal*, rinsed separately under running water in a colander, are left to dry on a flat surface for about fifteen minutes. This process makes them easier to cook and, anyway, in Bengal, we never cook anything without rinsing it first in water. While they dry I put on the kettle so that I have ready the hot, though not boiling, water you need to add to the *khichuri*. I heat the oil in a medium-sized, heavy-bottomed deep cooking pot, add the *garom mashla* and bay leaves and wait for a couple of minutes, without stirring them, for the fragrance to be released by the heat before I throw in the cumin seeds and chopped ginger. These I stir-fry for a couple of minutes, then add the half-dried rice and fry it for two to three minutes. Finally I add the roasted *moong dal* and the turmeric and stir the mixture for another two to three minutes before pouring on the hot water. The level of water should generally be 4 cm (1½ in) over the rice and *dal*. If necessary, more hot water can be added towards the end, depending on how thin you like your *khichuri* or whether the rice and *dal* are sticking to the pot. Adding a lot of water at the beginning will make a mishmash of the grains. Once the water comes to a boil, I add 2 teaspoons of salt and 3 teaspoons of sugar, reduce the heat to low and cover the pot. Generally it takes about twelve to fifteen minutes for the *khichuri* to be ready. To avoid sticking and even the slightest burning, which ruins the flavour, I keep checking from time to time and stir the mixture thoroughly with a spatula. If needed, I add a little more hot water. After ten minutes of cooking, it is a good idea to test the grains of rice and *dal*. When they feel nearly ready, I throw in the green chillies, check for salt and sugar, wait till the consistency is just right, add 2 teaspoons of ghee and remove the pot from the stove. The earlier you add the chillies, the hotter the *khichuri* will be, for the stirring will blend them in.

This plain *khichuri* does not require much preparation and is quick and easy to make. Since left-over *khichuri*, both hot and cold, is also delicious, nobody worries too much about the quantities. A more sophisticated version, called the *bhuni khichuri*, which requires more frying and has the texture of a pilaf, is made either for guests or for the family when the cook has more leisure. The colour of simple *khichuri* is always yellow from the turmeric, but this version can be made without it, so that the natural whitey-brown tones of rice and roasted *moong dal* are kept. Richer in taste than plain *khichuri*, one cannot have too much of it.

For a **Bhuni khichuri** for three to four people, I generally take 500 g (1 lb) of rice and 250 g (½ lb) of roasted *moong dal*; 4 medium onions chopped fine; 2 teaspoons of ground ginger and 2 tablespoons of chopped ginger; *garom mashla* as for the simple *khichuri*, but crushed lightly; 3 bay leaves; 1 teaspoon of freshly ground cumin and 1 teaspoon of cumin seeds; 7–8 ground chillies; 120 g (4 oz) of raisins; 175 ml (6 fl oz) of ghee; salt and sugar to taste.

The rice and *dal* are rinsed and dried as before. Then I heat the ghee in the pot and throw in the cumin seeds with 2 bay leaves. As soon as they turn brown, I add the crushed *garom mashla* and, a minute later, the chopped onions and ginger. These are stir-fried till brown and the rice is added. I lower the heat to medium and stir and stir until the rice makes popping noises. Then I add the *dal*, fry a little more and pour in the hot water, enough to cover the contents and stay almost 2.5 cm (1 in) above. Again, one has to be careful with the water, particularly because this *khichuri* has to be dry and fluffy, not soggy and mushy. A little more water can always be added if needed. As soon as the water comes to the boil, I add 2 teaspoons of salt and 2 teaspoons of sugar and the green chillies, then lower the heat and cook, covered, for about five to six minutes. Check the salt and sugar balance at this point, adding more if needed, before adding the ground ginger and ground cumin as well as the raisins. I then add the remaining bay leaf, cover the pot tightly and reduce the flame to the barest minimum. If the *khichuri* looks too dry, this is the time to sprinkle more hot water over it. From time to time over the next four to five minutes, I shake – never stir – the covered pot carefully, so that the grains will not stick to the bottom. When done, the *bhuni khichuri* will be very fluffy and should give off a complex aroma, heavier than that of the simple *khichuri*.

Many people love to add extra dollops of ghee to their platefuls of simple *khichuri*, although in these days of cholesterol fears, lemon juice squeezed over the top is also used to add zest. The *bhuni khichuri*, however, has sufficient ghee and spices to need any extra seasoning.

Although *khichuri* is almost a complete meal in itself, most Bengalis would be disappointed not to have certain well-loved accompaniments: slices of aubergines or halves of *patols* deep-fried in oil, potatoes sliced thin and fried with a seasoning of *panch phoron*, dry red chillies and salt. On the non-vegetarian side there is the ubiquitous omelette and pieces of fried fish. Some people boil eggs and then deep-fry them crispy brown to serve with *khichuri*. And in Muslim Bangladesh, where *bhuni khichuri* (in many versions) is very common, a dry but highly-seasoned meat dish will be served with it.

As the rains of Asharh continue – sometimes violent, at other times steady, or even stopping from time to time – the leaves of plants washed clean of summer dust and grime display their vigorous greenery. But the welcome greyness of clouds shielding the sun reminds you that this is no second spring. Rows of red-blossomed Krishnachura trees throw into relief the dense masses of clouds, whose lowering darkness is said to be the colour of the skin of Krishna, the Hindu deity.

Fairly early in Asharh comes Ambubachi, three days which mark the beginning of the monsoon proper according to ancient myths. Even if the monsoon has not appeared before this, even if the rains have begun and stopped, the skies have to open and mingle with the earth during these three days, for legend says that the fluid flow of red or brown earth mingled with rainwater at this time is a ritual bleeding of the earth presaging fertility.

Ambubachi is serious business for orthodox Hindus. In times gone by, even the two primary activites of the élite and the peasantry were forbidden. Brahmins were not allowed to pursue their study of the Vedas and the peasants had to refrain from ploughing the land, a practical directive since the three days of rain would leave the earth soft and receptive to cultivation. The change in the appearance of the land, from the gaping, fissured cracked earth of late summer, to the spongy, moist darkness of soil is amazing. Farmers can hardly wait to take their ploughs and oxen into the fields and get ready to sow their crops.

Hindu widows were not allowed to cook any food during Ambubachi and rice was absolutely forbidden them. I used to see my widowed grandmother and several other elderly widows in neighbouring houses make their preparations for these three days. They would prepare *luchis* and several vegetable dishes in advance and lay in a stock of fruits and home-made sweet yoghurt to be eaten with *chira*, flattened rice. Puffed rice (*muri*) and popped rice (*khoi*) were also permitted, as were home-made sweets. East Bengali Hindus are, however, more rigorous about widows' rituals. For them even pre-cooked food is taboo during Ambubachi. The widowed grandmother of a schoolfriend of mine used to sustain herself for three whole days on the pulp and juice of mangoes and ripe jackfruits, together with milk, yoghurt, *muri* and *khoi*. The occasional salted slices of cucumber or soaked chick-peas with chopped ginger provided some variety.

The only positive aspect I could find about Ambubachi for widows was that they could, with some freedom, drink milk, which was usually reserved for children and very old people in the average middle-class household. Milk is rarely drunk chilled in Bengal. I always found it interesting to see my grandmother add handfuls of *khoi* to the bowl of hot milk and see them float with mild popping sounds, or squeeze in the juice and pulp of a mango which turned the milk a vivid saffron yellow. The heat of the milk accentuated the strong smell of mango and I would inevitably stand over the bowl and sniff as hard as I could to enjoy the heady fruitiness to the full. But widows were not allowed to heat milk during Ambubachi, so my grandmother made do with *kheer* which had been prepared prior to Ambubachi. Folklore also says that drinking milk during Ambubachi provides immunity from snakebites, no mean advantage in rural Bengal where the fields and the villages can be luxuriant death-traps with lurking cobras and kraits.

Soon after Ambubachi comes Rathajatra, the first religious festival of the monsoon. Literally translated, Rathajatra means a chariot trip or journey. The story goes that when the Lord Jagannatha, a later incarnation of Krishna, was a child, he and his brother Balaram and his sister Subhadra decided to visit their aunt to convalesce from a bout of monsoon fever. After a week's visit, the three returned home, fully restored to health. The most elaborate celebration of Rathajatra takes place in the town of Puri in Orissa, where there is a huge temple of Jagannatha. A gigantic wooden chariot is constructed each year, the images of the three deities placed inside and priests and devotees combine to hold the huge rope attached to the chariot and pull it along to a predetermined destination. In the past, often many people would be crushed to death under the wheels of this moving contraption, not just by accident, but also because people believed that to die that way ensured an entry into heaven and freedom from the cycle of rebirth. The English word 'juggernaut' is not only a transliteration of Jagannath but derives its meaning from such incidents of self-immolation. Neighbouring Bengal has also adopted the chariot festival as her own, partly because the story of the gods as children echoes the other Bengali folktales about the childhood of Krishna. This is another day when it is supposed to rain, but no one minds because rain on Rathajatra presages a good monsoon.

At home the mandatory item of food on this day is *papor* or *papadam*, thin pale yellow or creamy white sheets of dried powdered *dal* (sometimes spiced) or rice flour, fried and served at lunch with *khichuri* and vegetables. The rice *papors*, creamy white in colour, were meant more for children than for adults because they were quite bland. I always liked to watch them being fried and would stand in the kitchen to watch my mother pick up the thin desiccated slices of *papor* and throw them in the hot oil. They immediatley puffed up and crinkled into fascinating curves and she would lift them out carefully to avoid breaking or browning them too much. In our house fish, meat or eggs were strictly forbidden on this day, but it was no hardship. We would sit in front of our platefuls of steaming, fragrant *khichuri*, the green chillies and the brown cinnamon or bay leaf standing out against the yellow background, waiting for Keshto, the cook, to come and serve fried slices of aubergine, potatoes, *patols* or even pumpkin. These I would arrange ceremoniously on my plate around the *khichuri*, the orange pumpkin, the dark brown aubergine and the greenish brown *patol*, forming a lovely unity of colour. As I squeezed lemon juice over the *khichuri*, Keshto would come again with a huge bowlful of crisply fried *papors* which disappeared almost in a flash.

The excitement of Rathajatra is mostly for children. In the evening, after the thrill of pulling our own mini-chariots up and down the long verandas, my cousins and I would be taken to the nearest *mela*, or fair, which began on the evening of Rathajatra and continued for nearly two weeks. Normally, food cooked at fairs or roadside stalls was strictly forbidden in my well-guarded childhood, but this was an evening for indulgence and we were usually taken out, not by parents, but by Patolmama, an old friend of my uncles, a confirmed bachelor with a heart of gold, who could refuse a child nothing. Tingling with anticipation, we would walk through the bright lights, past the rows of men sitting in front of their clay stoves with huge black *karais* on top, for heart-stopping rides on various merry-go-round contraptions. Later we could come back and join the jostling crowd shouting out orders for their *tele bhajas*, crispy snacks fried in oil: *beguni*, aubergine slices dipped in a batter of spiced *dal* powder and deep-fried, or *alur chop*, rounded balls of spiced mashed potatoes covered in the same batter. As I peeped from behind Patolmama's back, the hissing and bubbling of the oil, and the heat, smell and smoke in the inadequate light of hanging lanterns and kerosene lamps almost lifted the scene out of reality. With a delicious shiver I would stare hypnotised into the *karai* full of hot oil, remembering popular descriptions of hell where sinners are supposed to be fried in cauldrons of oil exactly like *begunis* or *alur chops*.

Away from the hot and sticky frying smell of the food stalls, the fragrance of *beli* and *jui*, two jasmine-like flowers, would lie heavily in the deep evening air. For the fair is traditionally one of the year's biggest gathering of plant sellers, with specimens ranging from rare or beautiful flowering plants for pots to specially bred cuttings of mango, lime or lychee trees.

The true beauty of Bengal in Shraban, the second month of the monsoon season, is to be found only in the villages where the fertility of the earth co-exists with the threat of engorged rivers that can later become wantonly, cruelly destructive. Amazingly, neither the rural landscape nor the pattern of agricultural life has changed much over time. Once the earth has been softened by the Asharh rains, the farmers plough their fields and plant the most important crop of the year, the Aman rice crop. The scanty summer planting, the Aush rice, has also benefited from the rain and stands firm in the fields to be harvested quietly around August. But most of the land is devoted to the all-important moonsoon planting, around which rural life and economy revolve.

The two primary categories of cooked rice are the *siddha*, or parboiled rice, and the *atap* rice, untouched by heat. Each will include rice of varying degrees of fineness and length. Parboiled rice keeps better and is more nutritious, which is probably why it is commonly used for lunch and dinner. The harvested rice is parboiled, dried in the sun and husked before marketing and storage. *Atap* rice is used for specific purposes such as the cooking of *polao, khichuri* and *payesh*, as well as being made into rice flour with which the Bengali makes a host of *pithas*, sweet and savoury. Among Hindus *atap* rice is also considered more appropriate for widows who are forced to be vegetarians and are constrained by numerous rules. The finer varieties of *atap* rice are usually saved for *payesh* or rice pudding and pilafs and Muslim *biryanis*, while the coarser ones are used for plain rice. In Chittagong, in Bangladesh, for instance, the local preference is for *atap* rice, even for daily meals.

Differences of soil, altitude and other factors also produced variations in the quality of rice from district to district in Bengal. The terrain in Bangladesh, say experts, is such that 10,000 varieties of rice can be grown there. While this potential is far from being realised, certain strains of rice acquired a special reputation. Barisal became famous for its *balam* rice, which is one of the tastiest and longest-grained varieties of parboiled rice in Bengal. But one has to be a Bengali, nurtured on rice for generations, to feel enthusiastic appreciation of this rice. For the uninitiated, there might well be no difference between packaged rice grown in the US or imported Patna rice and the *balam* which is growing rarer with time or the many kinds of fine-grained *ataps*.

Another important consideration behind the cooking of daily rice is texture. Traditionally, Bengali cooks drain the water in which rice has been cooked and parboiled rice is preferred because it is firmer than *atap* rice and also because it loses less of its nutritional value. Bengalis also have a distinct preference for old, stored rice, both parboiled and *atap*. Newly harvested rice is found to be more sticky and less firm. For *khichuri* or *polao*, where the rice is first fried, old *atap* rice is preferred because the grains, having lost all moisture, absorb the oil better. This greater fluffiness of texture also gives it a more voluminous appearance, hence the Bengali saying 'Old rice increases in the cooking,' which is also applied to tried and trusted servants and friends.

The abundance of the rice crop has also led to the other mutations that had their own place in daily life and ritual. Puffed rice, *muri*, became a favourite occasional snack as well as breakfast food served with milk and brown sugar. Popped rice, *khoi*, apart from being eaten with milk, is used to make a favourite winter sweet, *moa*. It also has a distinctly auspicious significance, unlike puffed rice, for it is poured into the sacred fire in front of which the Hindu wedding takes place, as a special offering to the gods. This, of course, is not peculiar to Bengal, but part of the pan-Indian Aryan culture.

To most outsiders, however, the most interesting mutation is the flattened rice, *chira*. Like *muri* and *khoi*, this, too, is made all over India, the unhusked rice being boiled longer than for parboiling and then flattened by being pounded forcefully. The husk separates from the grain during the pounding to reveal a paper-thin white grain with irregular edges. The fineness of the *chira* depends both on the quality of the rice and the art of the people making it. Probably no other region does as much with the *chira* as Bengal does. Soaked in water and softened, it is eaten with sugar, fruits, yoghurt or milk as *phalahar*. Combined with the coastal bounty of finely-ground coconut, it provides the most delicate of tastes. It can be fried very quickly in hot ghee or roasted in a dry pot, to be eaten as a savoury item seasoned with salt, pepper and chopped ginger. In winter it is combined with vegetables to make a quick *polao*, or with sticky-sweet date-palm sugar to make another kind of *moa*. Mixed with yoghurt and milk-based sweets, the *chira* becomes part of the offering for the gods, and brides and bridegrooms go through the ceremony of *dadhimangal* very early on their wedding day when they are given this to eat before the day's fast begins.

Given the all-pervasive presence of rice, the mother of all these inventions, it is easy to understand the eagerness with which the Bengali peasant looks forward to the monsoon, when he can put all his energy and labour into the sowing of this crop. The seeds are broadcast by hand over the receptive land and shoot up thickly in no time. Then comes the meticulous, back-breaking labour of transplanting the seedlings in carefully spaced rows. Men and women forget their differences as they stoop, ankle-deep in water, pressing in the seedlings with the ease of much practice. Though the monsoon helps to make the land ready, too much rain or violent winds can cause infinite disasters. So the farmers who long for the rain also pray for moderation. By the end of Shraban or a little later, the fields are full of the vivid emerald green of the standing rice crop, and then the beauty and promise of the sight is compensation enough for all their labour.

Once, around this time, I made the overnight journey by steamboat from Dhaka to Barisal, from where we took the boat to my husband's home village of Dapdapia in Nalchite thana. On my previous visit in the winter, we had travelled on from the landing jetty by *kutcha* or earthen roads, but this time the roads had all disappeared under water. As we glided along the numerous little canals, the well-grown rice plants on both sides nodded and shivered as the moving water touched their feet. In places the water almost disappeared and the boat somehow scraped through a mass of vegetation. The green leaves and budding ears of rice touched my face sharply, sometimes replaced by the softness of the luxuriant *kalmi*, a water-reed that is a favourite monsoon vegetable.

For me, it was a journey made magic by the sound of oars in the water, the rustle of leaves as we advanced through them and the intensity of a green earth under a threatening sky. The slow journey seemed of infinite duration, evoking all the fairy-tales my grandmother used to tell me of the *rakshashi*, demon queen, whose vital spark lay in the shape of a black hornet inside a box, down, down below the waters of a huge lake. I would sit enthralled as she told me of the nights when the queen assumed her true shape and went out of the palace to devour horses and elephants and even unwary human beings; of the prince, her stepson, who discovered her identity and fled from her pursuing hands and tongue; of his watery journey down, down to the hornet which he brought up to the land and killed, all in one breath, thus finding deliverance for himself and his father's kingdom.

Once we had arrived at the homestead of Kadam Bhai, a landowner farmer and long-time family friend, we had a simple and delicious lunch. The high point of the meal was a dish combining *dhenki shak*, a feathery fern-like green quite unfamiliar in Ghoti households like ours, and tiny shrimps. Rarely seen in the markets of Calcutta, *dhenki shak* grows mostly in East Bengal, Assam and the northern hilly areas of West Bengal. Its beauty lies in the head, where the 30 cm (1 ft) long stem bends forward gracefully into a hook and coils to an end. In many places this appearance has earned the *shak* the name of *boudaga shak*, *bou* meaning bride and *daga* being the tip. The analogy obviously derives from the blushing Bengali bride, her head covered with her sari, demurely bending forward.

Kadam Bhai's daughter, Shefali, had added tiny cubed potatoes and shrimps to the chopped *dhenki shak* and seasoned it with pungent ground mustard – complemented by mustard oil – freshly-ground coconut, green chillies, turmeric and salt. Though I know it is absolutely impossible to duplicate the delicate taste of *dhenki shak*, the other ingredients, available in the West, can be combined with chopped spring onions and potatoes to produce a different but equally delicious dish.

For **Spring onions with shrimps and coconut,** take 500 g (1 lb) spring onions chopped into 2.5 cm (1 in) lengths (including the onions at the bottom) and a handful of shrimps which have been dusted with turmeric and salt and lightly fried. Peel and cut 2 medium potatoes into 2.5 cm (1 in) long, thin slices and brown them lightly in oil. Apart from this you need 1 tablespoon of ground mustard seeds, 3 tablespoons of ground coconut, 2–3 green chillies and

salt. Heat 3 tablespoons of mustard oil in a *karai*, throw in
the spring onions, add a teaspoon of salt and keep covered
for a couple of minutes. When you uncover the *karai*, a lot
of moisture will have oozed out. Keep on a high flame, add
the ground mustard, stir for a minute or so, add the fried
shrimp, browned potatoes, coconut and green chillies, stir
thoroughly for three to four minutes and keep covered over
a low flame until the flavours are blended, the potatoes are
tender and all the moisture has evaporated. Before
removing, stir over high heat so that the dish becomes very
dry and check the salt, adding more if needed. As a side
dish, along with other items to be eaten with rice, this
should be enough for four people.

In our watery land Barsha is the time for eating all kinds of
other lush leafy greens. The *kalmi* growing beside the water is
a common favourite. Chopped fine, it is stir-fried with the five
spices (*panch phoron*), dry red chillies and lots of chopped
garlic. In the West spinach can be made in the same way with
or without the *panch phoron*, but the mustard oil is essential.
In the fields can be seen stretches of *shushni shak*, whose deep
velvety green soothes the eye just as the *shak* itself is supposed
to soothe you to sleep. Another succulent green, the *puishak*,
seems to have no Western substitute that can emulate its
slightly slippery, slightly astringent taste. Yet another strange
vegetable that Bengalis go crazy about is *kachu shak*, the long,
hollow stems (not leaves) of a kind of taro which, when
cooked, become a pulpy mush and readily absorb the flavour
and taste of other ingredients added to them. Asparagus,
boiled long enough, might be an equivalent in terms of delicate
flavour and texture. *Kachu shak* is an ideal combination for
small shrimp or the head of a fish, and there is also an
extraordinarily delicious vegetarian dish made by spicing the
boiled *shak* with whole bay leaves, ground cumin, chilli,
turmeric and some coconut, the whole being flavoured with
ghee before being removed from the fire. Little brown pre-
cooked chick-peas are usually added to this preparation.

Though now available throughout the year, the pumpkin is at its most prolific during the rains. It is so commonplace that most Bengalis consider it a native vegetable, but in reality it is probably a seventeenth-century import resulting from the Portuguese trade. The supposition finds some confirmation in the fact that in colonial times the pumpkin was referred to as the *biliti* or English *kumro*, just as the tomato was called the *biliti begun*, English aubergine. The indigenous *kumro*, similar to the white gourd, acquired the name of *chal kumro*, pumpkin on the roof, to distinguish it from its orange cousin.

Various of the tastier pumpkin dishes can be eaten with impunity by the strictest Hindu vegetarians. One very easy way to deal with it is to fry whole cumin seeds, chopped onions and green chillies, add the cubed pumpkin to it and sauté it till soft and edible. Fried shrimp can also be added to this.

 Pumpkin with coconut is more laborious since the pumpkin needs grating. For six people 1 kg (2 lbs) pumpkin, half a coconut, 1½ teaspoons of ground coriander, 1 teaspoon of ground cumin seeds, 1 teaspoon of chilli powder, 2 teaspoons of sugar and salt to taste, 120 ml (4 fl oz) of milk, 3–4 bay leaves, 1 teaspoon of *garom mashla* and 4 tablespoons of cooking oil are required. Grate the entire portion of the pumpkin. Grate the coconut and set aside. Heat some oil in the *karai* and put in the grated pumpkin. When it is half-fried, add the grated coconut. When the mixture turns brown, blend all the ground spices except *garom mashla* with the milk and add to the pumpkin. Keep stirring until all the moisture evaporates. Add the *garom mashla* before removing. If the oil seems inadequate for the frying, a little more can be added before the spices are put in.

Among the other monsoon vegetables that Bengalis love are varieties of *kachu* or taro. The king of the *kachu* kingdom is the *maan kachu*, often called just *maan*, which also means prestige or repute in Bengali. An enormous tuber, sometimes weighing as much as 15 kg (33 lbs), it is treated with the respect deserved by its repute. This has been strengthened by Ayurvedic theories ascribing to the *maan* the capacity to purify the blood, thus curing common afflictions like boils, sores and skin diseases. In our house for many years the pieces of *maan* bought from the market were simply boiled and mashed with salt and mustard oil. Green chillies could be added too, and, occasionally, the spiced oil from the pickle jar. Later, a Bangal friend showed us the greater novelty of eating it uncooked. The portion of *maan* was coarsely ground on the stone and the juice discarded. The fibre was then ground a second time with coconut, mustard seeds, green chillies and salt. The smooth paste was seasoned with pungent mustard oil.

Thankfully, some Bengali vegetables are better travelled. The banana tree, so loaded with myth and symbol in the folk-life of Bengal, provides two of Bengal's most cherished vegetables: the blossom, *mocha*, and the inner core of the trunk, *thor*. Although the trunk is not available elsewhere, banana blossom, neatly packed in tins, is imported from the Philippines and other South-East Asian countries to the ethnic shops of the West. Medieval Bengali literature is full of references to both *thor* and *mocha* being cooked and presented to Chaitanya (founder of the Bhakti cult) by his disciples. The tactile and visual pleasure of watching the magenta spathes of the *mocha* being pulled back to expose the baby bananas nestling underneath, of removing them in bunches and pulling out the hard central stem and the translucent fibre in front is lost with the canned product, but much time is saved and one avoids having one's fingers blackened with the juice which has to be discarded by boiling the chopped *mocha* before cooking. The taste of canned *mocha*, however, is far inferior to that of the fresh product, and I have often wondered why a Bengali entrepreneur does not try to import fresh *mocha* into Britain or the United States, along with the large numbers of bananas brought into both countries.

To feed four people with **Mochar ghanto**, you need 500 g (1 lb) of freshly chopped *mocha*, cooked and drained; 60 g (2 oz) of chick-peas soaked overnight or lightly cooked; 175 g (6 oz) of ground coconut; 2 medium potatoes, peeled and cubed; 1 teaspoon of cumin seeds for the *phoron*; 1 teaspoon of ground *garom mashla*; 4 tablespoons of oil and 1 tablespoon of ghee; salt and sugar to taste. Mix half of all the ground spices except the *garom mashla* thoroughly with the cooked *mocha* and set aside. Heat the oil in a *karai* or pot (aluminium, not iron, which reacts adversely with *mocha*), fry the potatoes light brown, remove and set aside. In the same oil throw in the *phoron*, fry for a couple of minutes and add the pre-soaked chick-peas and the rest of the ground spices minus the *garom mashla*. Keep stirring for two to three minutes, and add the spiced cooked *mocha*. Stir again for a few minutes, add the potatoes, stir for three to four minutes more and pour in 120 ml (4 fl oz) of water. Keep covered over a medium heat. When the water has almost evaporated, add the ground coconut, 2 teaspoons of salt and 4 teaspoons of sugar. The sweetness has to be a little pronounced. Stir well, taste and mix in a pinch of flour before removing from the stove. Mix the ghee with the *garom mashla*, add to the *mocha*, stir thoroughly and leave covered until it is time to serve. In a traditional meal, the *mochar ghanto* is eaten with rice after the fried vegetables and *dal* have been eaten and before any fish or meat dish.

After the attenuation of summer, the myriad rivers of Bengal swell joyously under the copious rainfall of Asharh and Shraban. Replenished, they cast off their previous lethargy and flow merrily on, the waves glinting in the occasional sunlight from behind the clouds. It is an invitation to the fishermen, Bengal's boat people. As the evening shadows lengthen, they start off, usually in pairs or small groups, in their fishing boats to haul in the silver catch all through the night. The Bengali *majhi*, boatman, has existed as a figure in many folktales and folksongs through the centuries and he is also the hero of Manik Bandyopadhyay's classic, *Boatman of the Padma*. Like his predecessors and successors, Bandyopadhyay's boatman comes back in the early hours of the morning under the faint light of a crescent moon in a sky filled with broken clouds. The light from the boatman's lantern illuminates the hold where the night's haul of hilsa – the monsoon's most prized and available fish – lies dead. This delicate fish does not live long out of water, but even in death its beauty is not destroyed. The silver scales gleam in the lamplight and the unblinking eyes resemble blue gems.

The monsoon is so associated with the *ilish*, called hilsa by the British, that Bengalis have given the name *ilshe guri* to the lacy mist of rain which replaces the heavy downpour of the first month, *ilshe* being the adjectival derivative of *ilish* and *guri* meaning grain or powder. The hilsa's life-cycle is something like that of the salmon. After starting life in the sea, the fish comes to spawn in the estuarine waters where the rivers meet the Bay of Bengal, and slowly moves upstream into northern India, growing in size up to 2.5 kg (5½ lbs). Many of the hilsa caught during the monsoon are big with roe, which is a delicacy in its own right and considered a caviar of the tropics. When taken out of the fish, the roe resembles two elongated kidneys, joined at the top, brownish in colour with innumerable black veins showing in the enclosing membrane. It can vary in length according to the time and the size of the fish, but is rarely more than 15 cm (6 in). When fried or whipped and cooked with spices, it has a lovely, chewy graininess imbued with the characteristic hilsa flavour. But the bigger the roe, the less tasty the fish.

All the differences between Ghotis and Bangals, between Hindus and Muslims, disappear in an agreement of amity – that there is nothing to rival the hilsa. Friendly disputes arise again over which is the superior: the hilsa from the Ganga by which the West Bengalis swear, or the hilsa from the Padma over which Bangladesh drools. Padma specimens can be much bigger than those from the Ganga, though in terms of flavour and softness of texture, according to the proportion of oil in the fish, the Ganga variety is the superior of the two to my mind, but perhaps that is my Ghoti bias.

Expatriate Bengalis in the West have tried various fishes in their desperate nostalgia for the hilsa, and the one that most of them think comes closest to their unique fish is the shad. In shape and size it is certainly a fair equivalent, but the flavour and taste of the hilsa are unique. For the real pleasure of eating this 'darling of the waters', as a Bengali poet called it, you have to come to Bengal, East or West. When you do, you must be prepared to eat with your fingers, for the hilsa's treacherous bones can lodge themselves in the throat of the unwary. I once heard an American in Dhaka compare Bengali women to the hilsa: 'Very tempting on the outside, but try to get close and you choke on the bones'. His comment prompted me to reflect that some people deserve their bones.

In its preparation, too, the hilsa breaks all rules. All other fish are repeatedly washed and cleaned thoroughly of blood and slime before they are cooked. Blood, in fact, is anathema in food. For the Muslims, blood is *haram*, or absolutely repugnant. They make sure that even their meat is drained of blood by severing the arteries in the neck of the animals and birds before actually killing them. And though the Hindus slaughter their animals without such refinements, they too are careful to wash all traces of blood from their fish or meat before cooking. But when it comes to the hilsa, many Bengalis will wash the fish only once, after the head and guts have been removed, even though a lot of blood oozes out subsequently as the fish is cut into pieces. By some strange logic, the blood is supposed to confer added delectation. I was amazed by the sight of a Bangladeshi Muslim friend of mine in Dhaka treating her hilsa this way. Even her mother, a devout Muslim lady, stood looking on as if nothing extraordinary was happening.

Once the head and guts have been removed and the body scaled, the hilsa is halved lengthwise along the spine, but the cut stops 10 or 12.5 cm (4 or 5 in) above the tail where the body becomes too narrow. The tailpiece is then separated

and set aside. The two longitudinal halves are cut
horizontally into pieces as thick as you want, usually 2.5 cm
(1 in) or so. The *peti* or stomach portion has large bones and
the flesh is more oily, which makes it the more prized portion,
but the *daga* or back portion is very good crisply fried or in a
jhol combined with vegetables. It is much more bony,
though, and requires concentration to eat without mishap.

There are recipes enough for the hilsa to fill an entire book.
Individuals, families and regions have all developed their
special styles, spices and combinations for this delightful fish.
Here I will mention only a few that are my favourites and
also very easy to make. All of them can be tried in the West
with various hilsa substitutes: shad, salmon and even herring.
Though the mackerel is also a soft and oily fish, somehow I
do not find it satisfying in a Bengali recipe. The simplest and
one of the best ways to have hilsa is to fry it. Once the pieces
are washed and cleaned, they are dusted with some salt and
powdered turmeric and left for a few minutes before being
fried to a rich, deep brown in mustard oil. A good hilsa will
release almost 120 ml (4 fl oz) of oil in the process of frying.
Herring fried in this way is particularly good, though it may
not yield as much oil. Bengalis treasure the hilsa oil, pouring
it over piping hot servings of rice and mixing it in thoroughly
so that the fish can be eaten with this reinforced flavour. All
you need to accompany this is a pinch of salt on the side and
one or more green chillies, according to your taste for hot
food, from which you take the occasional bite. If, however,
you are serving the fish with *khichuri*, or if there are lots of
other items for which you want to save the rice, then you
store the fish oil carefully, for it is an invaluable flavouring
agent for vegetables, especially those cooked together with
the hilsa head. The one I liked best was *puishak*, the slightly
slippery-textured greens which miraculously absorbed and
enhanced the hilsa flavour. Another classic Bengali
preparation for the hilsa, *shorshe ilish*, is simple and depends
on a single predominant taste, that of mustard.

For **Shorshe ilish** (or hilsa with mustard) for four people, you need 500 g (1 lb) of *peti* pieces. A big fish will give you eight or nine pieces. These should be washed and cleaned thoroughly. Grind 1½ tablespoons of pungent black mustard seeds with a touch of salt and a green chilli. This will dispel the bitterness of the mustard. Indian shops in the West always sell this mustard and it is worthwhile going to the trouble of buying it, for white or brown mustard is no acceptable substitute. The whole point of the dish is its pungency which complements the rich oiliness of the fish. Mustard seeds can be ground in a blender, though not as finely as on a grinding stone. Take 7–8 green chillies (or 2–3 if you cannot tolerate too much) and slit them down the middle. Rub the pieces of fish with salt and turmeric. Heat 4 tablespoons of mustard oil in a *karai* and add the mustard paste together with ½ teaspoon of turmeric powder. Stir for a couple of minutes and add 250 ml (8 fl oz) of water. As soon as it comes to the boil, gently put in the hilsa pieces and the green chillies. Cover and cook for ten minutes over a medium flame. Uncover and taste to determine how much extra salt is needed. The water should evaporate sufficiently to leave the fish coated in a thick, grainy, yellow sauce when you remove it. If you want a thinner sauce, you can add some more water. Remove from the stove and add a little fresh mustard oil to the fish. Leave covered for a few minutes. When you serve it with plain boiled rice the sharp taste of the mustard will hit the palate. The important thing to remember, I find, is not to overcook the fish. The stomach pieces, in particular, are very soft and oily and too much heat will destroy the texture, if not the flavour. As with most Bengali dishes, there is always room for experiment and adjustments. Some people prefer more of the mustard paste than others, while some love to drown their fish in mustard oil.

A similar way of preparing the fish – more common in East than in West Bengal – is called a *paturi* from the word *pata*, which is Bengali for leaf.

For this **Ilish paturi**, take the pieces of fish, clean them and mix them thoroughly with salt, turmeric, the ground mustard, green chillies and a liberal helping of mustard oil. The whole mixture is then wrapped in banana leaves and the packet tied with string before it is thrust among the dying embers of a clay oven, or toasted on a *tawa* or flat pan over a low heat. The packet is turned over several times. By the time the top layer of leaf is burnt black, the fish should be ready. The process can also be duplicated in an oven set at 150°C (330°F, gas mark 1). In the absence of banana leaves, aluminium foil can be used. Once the fish is cooked, it should be removed from the wrappings and all the sauce scraped out with a spoon. The moisture and oil from the fish combined with the mustard paste and oil will produce quite a bit of sauce.

During my childhood and college years in Calcutta, I had heard my relatives speak of the 'strange' ways the East Bengalis sometimes treated their hilsa, but I had never encountered any recipes that seemed particularly *outré*. It was only after I went to live in Bangladesh that I came across some of the less usual forms of preparing hilsa. A cook I hired in Dhaka, who came from the Bangladesh district of Mymensingh, was the first person to serve me hilsa with coconut milk. Though Sabu the cook had the maniacal appearance of true genius and had already proved his worth in the kitchen, even I was at first a bit sceptical about how this dish was going to turn out. The daring idea (or so it seemed to my timid West Bengali mind) of combining unlikely items like onions and ghee with hilsa (fish is always cooked in mustard oil, and Ghotis never use onion with hilsa) seemed to me fraught with disastrous possibilities. But Saba had already demonstrated his mastery of unusual combinations, and so I allowed him to experiment with a plump and expensive hilsa. When I finally served the dish, I was charmed by the novelty and richness of the taste.

To make **Hilsa with coconut milk** for four people, you need 500 g (1 lb) of hilsa *peti*. The *daga* can also be used, but since the fish will not be fried, it will be harder to pick the bones out of the soft flesh. You also require: 1 lemon; a whole coconut from which to extract milk, or you can sub- stitute tinned coconut milk imported from South-East Asian countries into the West, the quantity needed being 250 ml (8 fl oz); 7–8 medium onions; a 4 cm (1½ in) piece of ginger; 4–5 green chillies; 2 dry red chillies; 120 ml (4 fl oz) of ghee; *garom mashla* consisting of 3 sticks of cinnamon and 4 whole carda- moms; salt to taste. Wash the pieces of hilsa, but do not add salt or turmeric. Extract the milk from the coconut by cutting out pieces from the shell, grinding them in a blender, mixing it with some hot water and squeezing out and discarding the fibre. You will need 250 ml (8 fl oz) of thick milk for the fish. Peel 2 of the onions and the piece of ginger and grind them to a paste with the red chillies. You can use only one chilli if you want. Squeeze all the juice out of the lemon into a bowl. Heat the ghee in a *karai* and add the *garom mashla*. After a couple of minutes, add the chopped onions and the green chillies. Fry till the mixture becomes reddish brown and add the ground onion and ginger and 2 teaspoons of salt. Add a quarter of the coconut milk and fry a little longer. When the contents start sticking to the pot, pour in the rest of the coconut milk and add the pieces of hilsa. Reduce the heat to low and simmer covered for twelve to fifteen minutes. Uncover to see if the fish is done and the salt is right. You may need to add some more. Pour in the lemon juice, stir gently and remove from the stove. This dish tastes much better with fine *atap* rice than parboiled rice. Wedges of lemon may also be served so that each person can adjust the tartness to his own taste.

Bangladesh also has its own recipes for hilsa roe. There I have seen the uncooked roe being put in a bowl and mashed thoroughly with a spoon or fork. The membrane disintegrates and is discarded and the granulated substance of the roe is seasoned with salt, turmeric and a little chilli paste or powder. One large potato is then peeled and chopped into tiny cubes and browned in mustard oil with a finely chopped large onion. Then the seasoned roe is added together with several slit green chillies. The entire mixture is stirred thoroughly until it turns into a brown-mustard grainy mass with the potatoes showing as tiny lumps. This increases the quantity of roe, which can become a side-dish for a family of four or five. My feudal friend from Tangail, Farhad Ghuznavi, also described the preparation made in his village by combining the hilsa roe with *karamcha*, a very sour local berry which has a semi-magical status, for a rural Bengali rhyme invokes *karamcha* with the leaves of lime trees as the potent combination for driving away rain.

A Bengali family can sometimes make an entire meal out of the different preparations of hilsa during the monsoon and find nothing strange about it. Sometimes we start with a *chhanchra* of hilsa head with green leafy vegetables served with the initial helping of rice. Then we take a fresh supply of hot rice, pour hilsa oil over it and have pieces of fried hilsa *daga*. This will be followed by the fried roe portioned out between family members. The *peti*, cooked in a pungent mustard sauce, will be the *pièce de résistance* that finishes the meal. Alternatively, one can start by pouring the hilsa oil over the rice and eating portions of the roe with it. This may be followed by a thin hilsa *jhol* with aubergines and potatoes, after which the richer taste of hilsa *peti* with coconut milk will taste wonderful.

Hilsa is not the only fish which produces its roe during the monsoon. The carp family – such as rui, katla, mirgel – all swell with eggs at this time, and in the bazaars both the fish and the roe are sold in separate portions so that you can buy as much of each as you wish. The roe of the rui is a favourite monsoon dish, as much because it is so easy to cook and so very tasty, as because it is a substantial source of not too expensive protein. Once the translucent covering membrane has been peeled away before cooking, the inner granules are seen to be slightly bigger than the hilsa roe's, grey and lumpish. Its texture, too, is dissimilar and needs a binding agent to hold it together. In these *boras*, fried balls made of carp roe, a little mashed potato lends a fluffy softness to the grainy roe and flour acts as a binder.

 To make **Carp roe boras** for four people, take 250 g (½ lb) of carp roe, wash away all traces of blood on the outer membrane, carefully peel it away and discard. Put the roe in a bowl and mix it with 2 teaspoons of freshly ground ginger, 1 medium onion chopped fine, 2 teaspoons of turmeric powder, 4–5 finely chopped green chillies, a small bunch of finely chopped mint leaves, 1 tablespoon of lemon juice and 2½ teaspoons of salt. Whip the roe very thoroughly until it is frothy. Boil 1 large potato and mash it to a fine smooth paste. Add this to the roe together with 2 heaped tablespoons of flour and mix thoroughly. Heat 60 ml (2 fl oz) of mustard oil in a *karai* and drop in the roe mixture, a large spoonful at a time. As the spoonfuls form into round balls, fry them brown on all sides before removing them.

These *boras* can be eaten fried like this as a savoury snack, appetiser or side-dish with rice and *dal*. Finding a substitute for this in the West may be difficult unless you can persuade your fishmonger to supply you with roe from the local varieties of carp. Shad roe, which is available, is simply not suitable because of its lesser bulk and delicacy of taste and texture.

Freshwater crabs are also plentiful in Bengal during the monsoon and usually bought for lunch on a Sunday or other holiday when one can have a leisurely meal and spend time prying the white flesh loose from the body and the claw. The Bengali crab is never very big, the entire body being no more than 7–10 cm (3–4 in) in diameter, the claws providing added dimension. They are medium grey in colour and the nearest equivalent in size in the West would be the American softshell crabs served in restaurants on the East coast in the summer. During the monsoon we prefer to buy a lot of females for the coral and a few males for the greater quantity of flesh in their claws. The flesh is flaky and quite soft, unlike that of crabs and lobsters from the ocean. Since we do not throw live crabs in boiling water to cook them, the fishmonger generally wrenches the claws from the body and cracks them in several places. The top shell is also removed by pounding it on a hard surface with a hammer. Before cooking, the bodies are cut into two or four pieces (according to size) and washed thoroughly, with the claws, in very hot water.

 To cook the crabs for **Crab jhal**, you need onions (chopped fine or ground to a paste), ground ginger, chilli and turmeric powder, ground mustard, 8–10 green chillies, salt and mustard oil. Dusted with salt and turmeric, the crabs have to be fried first in hot oil. The pieces of the body are put in so that the unshelled portions are facing downwards. This will help congeal the coral. A couple of minutes after putting in the bodies, the claws and legs are added and fried until they are bright red in colour. Then they are removed and set aside. The onions are then browned in the same oil, all the ground and powdered spices put in and the crabs returned to the pan. They are stirred over a high heat for six to eight minutes, then salt and green chillies are added with enough water to cover the crabs, the pan is covered and the crabs are cooked over a medium heat until they are done. Finally, the dish is finished over a high flame so that all the moisture evaporates and the spicy sauce coats the crabs. Ideally the spices should penetrate the cracks in the claws and flavour the flesh inside. This is usually served with plain boiled rice. *Garom mashla* can sometimes be substituted for the ground mustard for variety.

All this bounty from the rivers can make it easy to forget, especially in the safety of a daily urban existence, just how threatening the rivers can be during Barsha. But the same laughing waters that ensure the livelihood of numerous fishermen and are a source of the piscene variety which is the mainstay of Bengali cuisine can become a ruthless, destructive force, demonic in its mirth as it sweeps away everything in its path. Once in Bangladesh, at the end of Shraban, I was confronted with the full potency and terror of the rolling, raging waters. The rains had been fierce and unremitting and there were reports of floods from the southern districts. We, however, were going north, taking the ferry at Aricha where the rivers Jamuna and Padma meet. By the time the ferry appeared and all the waiting vehicles had got on, the August sky had darkened ominously, a gale-like wind had begun to tousle the surface of the river and the junction of the rivers seemed as wide and turbulent as the sea.

As we made our way, the storm intensified and the huge ferry rocked like the frailest of banana boats. Like the medieval heroine Behula who had placed her husband's corpse on a raft made of banana tree trunks and journeyed down the rivers to placate a vengeful goddess, I too felt I needed all the faith I could muster to reach my destination. Perversely, I got out of the jeep and stood on the deck of the ferry, wrapped in a flimsy sheet of plastic. Under my feet I was aware of the engines vibrating hard and fast, while the sheet of rain enveloped me, rent from time to time by furious streaks of lightning. Echoing through my panic, I could hear one of East Bengal's famous folksongs about a boatman and a merchant who are carrying valuable merchandise in a leaking boat caught in a storm. Reproachfully, the merchant laments that had he known how damaged his friend's boat was, he would never have entrusted himself and his goods to it. For now the heartless river was speaking in many tongues, each spelling doom, and all that could be seen in front was the golden girl who danced with bolts of lightning.

Bhadra, mid-August to mid-September, the last month of the monsoon, is by traditional reckoning part of early autumn or Sharat. Tagore depicted Bhadra as hovering between a dense, brooding melancholy and tumultuous outbursts before disappearing in a haze of sultry heat, but the reality is more an all-pervading humidity. Still the rains continue, sometimes inexorable, sometimes intermittent, sometimes violent. No chanted incantation about lime leaves and *karamcha* berries has any effect on the dreaded moisture falling, falling, falling. By now everyone is exhausted by the monsoon that was once so eagerly awaited. Even the poets give up. For them, Bhadra arouses only images of melancholy and despair. Radha, as depicted by the sixteenth-century poet Vidyapati, bemoans the emptiness of her world in Bhadra for Krishna has gone forever.

Everything is either coated with mildew or soggy with moisture and the few hours of sunshine here and there are used to air sheets, clothes and bedding. Even the bazaars are no longer much joy as customers jostle each other on wet, muddy floors and try to pick out vegetables that are not rotten or riddled with worms and fungus. Job Charnock, the intrepid British trader who is credited with founding Calcutta, had his first experience of the place during Bhadra. He arrived by boat on 24 August 1690 and the entry in his diary describes the monotonous dripping rain, the grey gloom and the men falling sick with tropical fever and dysentery.

Like the heat of the summer, the damp and humidity of the monsoon also take their toll on the system. Indigestion and diarrhoea are common as are colds and fever. Hot, sweet cups of tea are much in demand. At the slightest hint of a sniffling nose or sore throat and cough, the Bengali will demand tea, sometimes with the juice of ginger added as a remedy for colds. Like all popular remedies for illness, the cup of tea has become the pivot around which a whole series of images of the lazy Bengali *babu* has evolved. Since the drink is a direct result of our colonial experience, it is not surprising that many of the images come from stories about the British boss putting up with the inadequacy of his tea-loving clerk. The fellow is never found when needed; he has always just stepped out for tea. He never has time for work; he's too busy sneezing and coughing. And when there is a particular rush of jobs to be done, he's sure to have disappeared for the day, ostensibly laid up in bed with a fever, but actually enjoying the cosiest of *addas* in his favourite teashop.

The *adda* is not a food but one of the great Bengali

institutions. The nearest definition would be a regular gathering of friends or cronies, where everything under the sun is discussed threadbare. And no *adda*, at home or in the teashop, can be complete without tea, even in the height of summer. The Bengali teashop is usually an unpretentious place. In the villages or poorer urban neighbourhoods it may be nothing more than a tarpaulin or piece of bamboo matting stretched over four posts. Under this rude shelter will be a table, a couple of rickety benches and a portable stove with the kettle permanently on. The more respectable places will be like small one-room restaurants where groups of men will spend hours smoking and drinking cups of tea. The occasional loner will also be there, absorbed in his newspaper, and no one will hurry him over his tea and perusal. One of my favourite teashops, on the pavement running along a major thoroughfare in south Calcutta, is more a stall than a shop. The two portable stoves are almost next to the kerb and the small counter with shelves below has trolley-like wheels so that the owner can take it back home with him at night. Beyond this there is only provision for shelter over the owner's head, the two stoves behind him and two stools for the customers. But the lack of seating means nothing and the steady crowd grows from afternoon onwards, the customers standing thickly around this makeshift contraption or sitting on the steps of nearby houses, each enjoying small glasses of this man's special beverage – lemon tea with sugar and a pinch of *bitnoon*, a dark, pungent salt.

Sometimes, during Bhadra's oppressive rains, tea is all that you want and the loss of appetite is such that even hilsa loses its charm. This is when various chutneys are made, frequently as much for taste as for therapy. Coconut, *posto* or poppy seeds and mint leaves, ground with green chillies, tamarind, salt, sugar and fresh mustard oil, are used for fresh-tasting raw chutneys. The *karamcha* and the juicy *kamranga* or star fruit are cooked with roasted powdered *panch phoron* and a couple of dry red chillies, yielding their tartness into a thin sauce. One of the most delicious chutneys, served to the family as also to the guests at weddings, parties and funerals, is made with pineapple, which is a monsoon fruit in Bengal.

 Among the many recipes for **Pineapple chutney**, I particularly like this one. We take a nice ripe pineapple and peel and cut it into tiny cubes. The important thing is to throw out the hard central portion and to gouge out the eyes with a sharp knife. Half a coconut is grated. In a medium-sized aluminium *karai* 2½ tablespoons of ghee are heated and *garom mashla* consisting of 3 sticks of cinnamon, 3 cloves and 8–10 whole cardamoms are thrown in. (Some people grind the *garom mashla* coarsely before using it.) When the fragrance is released, the cubed pineapple, 60 g (2 oz) of raisins and 1 teaspoon of salt are added. These are stirred over a medium heat for four to five minutes before 1 l (1¾ pints) of water is added. A lot of water is needed to cook the pineapple and to leave some for the sauce. When the pineapple is tender to the point of being almost shredded, the coconut is added along with 250 g (8 oz) of sugar. The chutney is then cooked over a high heat for about five minutes. The salt and sugar are tested (more salt will probably be needed at this stage) and a teaspoon of flour blended with a little water is mixed into the chutney to give it a smooth texture. After a couple of minutes the chutney is removed from the stove. It is either chilled or served at room temperature, never hot. Bengalis do not eat chutney as a relish with other items of food. It is eaten at the end of a meal, sometimes with *papor* on the side, before dessert.

To relieve the aches and pains of monsoon flu, and prevent the monsoon sniffles, many traditional housewives, especially among the Bangals, swear by a concoction made with *kalo jeera* or onion seeds. Folk wisdom endows these little black seeds with miraculous qualities, from repelling moths in silk and woollen clothes to curing all kinds of digestive and bronchial ailments. This particular preparation, a little round pulp of spicy-hot relish, is also delicious with rice.

 To make **Kalo jeera bharta**, a teaspoon of *kalo jeera* is toasted on a flat pan or *tawa*. Then an entire head of garlic is taken, all the cloves peeled, rinsed and crushed roughly on the grinding stone. The garlic is then fried in a little ghee, together with 1 or 2 whole green chillies. Afterwards, the garlic, chillies, roasted *kalo jeera* are all ground together into a paste and fresh mustard oil and salt added. The relish is divided up between two or three people to be eaten with hot rice as a starter.

Despite the rain, gloom, debility of disease and threat of flood, the irrepressible Bengali spirit manages to find some occasion for joy and festivity in Bhadra. Even the heaviest rain acquires a benign significance on Janmashtomi, early in the month, because the birth of Krishna in prison on that date took place on a night of pouring rain, and it is believed that it will inevitably rain on Janmashtomi. I grew up listening to my grandmother telling me the thrilling tale of Krishna's father Vasudeb smuggling his infant son out of prison. The world outside was full of water, but Vasudeb struggled on, miraculously sheltered by the thousand-hooded king of serpents, Vasuki, and reached Gokul where he left the baby in the keeping of a dairy farmer, Nanda, and his wife, Jashoda. Had Krishna's whereabouts been discovered, he would have been killed by his Herod-like uncle Kamsa, who had been forewarned of death at the hands of a nephew.

For the devout Hindu, particularly the Vaishnavs, Janmashtomi is a day of total fasting. In the old days affluent households would organise non-stop singing of devotional songs for eight or 24 hours. As if to compensate for the rigours of such a day, custom decrees that one of the most glorious offerings of nature, the ripe palm or *taal*, should be eaten after Janmashtomi. The ripe *taal* cannot be eaten directly because of its fibrous content and the bitter element in its pulp. Once peeled, therefore, the fibrous sections of the fruit are rubbed against a woven surface to extract the thick saffron pulp and juice. It has a very strong, almost intoxicating aroma which fills the house and alerts the neighbours as well as the flies. The extract is then loosely tied up in a cloth and left hanging for as long as five or six hours, until the bitter juices have dribbled out.

The pulp is too cloyingly rich to eat by itself, so Bengalis have devised two methods to deal with it. One is to cook it slowly with milk and grated coconut to make a cremay *kheer*, one of the classics of East Bengal. The other, familiar to me from my own West Bengal childhood, is to mix it with both rice flour and wheat flour, as well as a bit of grated coconut, and fry it in the form of little round *boras*. There are no near equivalents for the extraordinary taste and flavour of *taal* pulp. Its full-bodied fruitiness resembles that of the mango, but has an extra honeyed quality which can make it oppressive if you absorb it for too long. But those lovely crunchy *boras*, brown on the outside and saffron inside, did not linger long enough to oppress anyone. I could well understand why a popular Vaishnav song visualised Nanda, the dairy farmer and Krishna's adoptive father, dancing gleefully as he consumed his *taal boras*.

For the last few days of Bhadra the sun tends to blaze in the sky and the earth gives up its moisture. The only clouds visible are the white and fleecy ones of autumn. The last Hindu festival of the season, appropriately, takes place on the *sankranti*, or last day of Bhadra when Bishwakarma, patron deity of aristans, skilled labourers, mechanics and all those who live by their hands, is worshipped in Bengal. He is our Vulcan, his name literally meaning the maker of the world, and all factories, presses and artisans' workshops remain closed in his honour, no matter how much the *babu* or the factory-owner may grumble. The women of the artisan communities observe Bishwakarma's day as *arandhan*, meaning without cooking. No fires are lit in their kitchens.

Instead, all the festive foods are prepared the day before in a fever of activity. And no matter how meagre its means, each family will buy and cook a hilsa, whose taste and quality is the subject of much discussion over the following days.

For children, Bishwakarma means kite-flying, the traditional expression of the conviction that the monsoon has really withdrawn. For real enthusiasts, this is no less serious than worshipping the god. Yards and yards of string are painstakingly coated with lethal powdered glass before being rolled on to double-handled spools. Once the kites are up, honour demands the hounding of all rivals, locking threads with them and trying to dislodge them with the superior abrasion of your thread. Victory, when it comes, is greeted with the resounding cry of '*Bho-katta!*' By the afternoon of the *sankranti* the multi-coloured kites chase the clouds and each other with all the fresh enthusiasm of liberated energy.

Sharat · Hemanta

EARLY AND LATE AUTUMN

An old Bengali proverb says that if the *kash* has started flowering, you know the rains are over and the autumn has begun. More than spring, it is this season, compounded of early autumn or Sharat and late autumn or Hemanta, that is a time of unalloyed hope. One more monsoon has been lived through. One more harvest awaits the grower of rice. In the countryside the white, broom-like *kash* flowers grow beside the ponds and rivers mirroring blue skies with fleecy white clouds.

The lush humidity of monsoon is slowly replaced with a gradual evaporation of moisture and the overwhelming, almost dank greenness of the landscape is transformed into a mixture of green, gold and brown. The *ata*, a fruit available specifically during this short and delightful season, symbolises the qualities of the Bengali autumn in appearance and flavour. Its hard, knobbly, green and black exterior is a surprising contrast to the fragrant creaminess of its flesh wherein nestle glossy black seeds. So tasty is the flesh that Bengalis do not mind the bother of having to spit out seeds after every mouthful. Like potatoes and tomatoes, the *ata* is of foreign origin, having been brought to India by Europeans. A native of Central and South America, the *ata* is called *chirimoya* in Spanish and, either imported or grown in Florida, is sometimes stocked in American supermarkets under the name of *cheremoyo*.

While the fields gleam with the ripened rice crop, in the cities and villages there is the splendour of the festive autumnal rites to come. The *kumors*, or potters, build life-sized straw and clay images of the goddesses Durga, Lakshmi and Kali, toiling to make each more brilliant in colour, each more vibrant with life. For the hour of the goddesses is now at hand and Bengal awaits them expectantly. Stepping daintily on rose-tinted feet, they come, one, by one, by one, to be worshipped in a blaze of light and sound and colour.

Ashtami, the second day of Durga's visit, is the most important day of the festival. In the morning everyone is supposed to fast, bathe and go over to the nearest place of worship where the priest chants special prayers to the goddess and the devotees repeat them while holding a small offering of flowers and special leaves that have to be thrown at the feet of the goddess. The entire ritual is repeated three times before you are free to go home and break your fast.

Even those who are lax during the year tend to obey the vegetarian restrictions of Ashtami, although these do not

mean austerity. For lunch we would have *khichuri* and at
dinner, after a whole afternoon and evening of tramping
around the city, visiting the goddesses in their canopied
enclosures called *pandals*, there would be round golden *luchis*,
puffed up like balloons. The evocation of Ashtami with the
drums beating and the bell ringing for the evening ritual of
arati performed before the goddess by the priest has a special
association in many Bengali minds with *luchis* and various
tasty vegetarian dishes.

Luchis are a kind of fried bread specially loved in Bengal
even though we are primarily rice eaters. In northern India a
similar bread is known by the name of *puri*. The main
difference between the *luchi* and the *puri* is that the former is
made out of the finest white flour while *puris* are made with
coarser whole wheat flour. In feudal households of the last
century *luchis* were often served with savoury vegetables
during afternoon tea. In appearance a *luchi* is a round golden
disk, 12.5–15 cm (5–6 in) in diameter, and puffed up like a
balloon with hot air. The flour is mixed with water and some
ghee and kneaded thoroughly before being separated into
small portions which are rolled out into flat disks for frying.
However, if a lot of oil or ghee is added to the dough while
kneading, the *luchi* also absorbs a lot of oil in the course of
frying. It becomes flaky instead of puffy and is known as a
khasta luchi. These are much too rich to eat on a regular basis.
There are many variations in the size of *luchis*. Some people
like making tiny ones, 7.5 cm (3 in) in diameter. In our home
we prefer them slightly bigger, about 12.5 cm (5 in) across.
Small or large, they need to be served as soon as possible after
being made. The ideal way is to have a supply of hot ones
coming from the kitchen as you eat, although that means a
rough deal for the cook. The frying pan is no substitute for the
karai, for *luchis* have to be deep-fried. A Chinese wok might
do, although being more shallow than the *karai*, it will need
more oil to start with. As the oil reduces with the frying, the
cook adds more, but it must always be heated well before the
next *luchi* is put in.

To make **Luchis** for half a dozen people, I usually take 500 g (1 lb) of flour, which makes five or six for each person. For big eaters you need more. I put the flour on a large tray or platter, preferably with raised sides, add 1 teaspoon of salt and 2½ teaspoons of ghee or peanut oil and mix them well. (You can make sure that the oil is sufficient by taking a handful of the flour and pressing it tightly in your fist. If the flour adheres in a lump, the oil is right; if it falls apart, mix in just a little more oil). After the oil has been well mixed in, the flour has to be kneaded into a dough with water. I generally start with 300 ml (10 fl oz) of water, which I keep adding slowly to the flour as I gather it in from all sides of the tray to make one lump. If you find you still need a little more water, then carefully sprinkle some over the dough. Too much will ruin the dough, making it too thin. Once the flour has become a neat lump, the hard work of kneading starts. The more you do this, the better the quality of dough and the puffier the *luchi*. Usually ten to twelve minutes of forceful kneading with both palms, pressing down with the base of the palm, is good enough. At the end, the dough should feel elastic when pulled apart. It is then divided into the little round portions called *nechis*. Each one is smoothed over between the palms and pressed to flatten it, then rolled out on the board as thin as possible to make a 12.5 cm (5 in) *luchi*. The traditional way is to dip the *nechi* into a bowl of oil and then roll it out so that it does not stick to the rolling board. However the oily surface can be slippery, and another way is to dust each *nechi* very lightly with flour before rolling. A perfect circle is hard to achieve, but that is the ideal. As I roll the *luchis* out, I keep them side by side on a large dry platter or sheet of newspaper spread on the kitchen counter. It is best not to let them overlap too much because they might start sticking to each other. Once seven or eight have been rolled out, I put the *karai* on the stove, heat 120 ml (4 fl oz) of peanut oil in it and start frying. To do this well, hold one side of a *luchi*, lower it gently into the oil – still holding it – and set it afloat like a paper boat. This way you avoid a splash and prevent the thin disk of flour from crumpling up. As it puffs up like a balloon, turn it over with a spatula, fry for a minute more and gently lift it up along the side to drain off all excess oil. A good *luchi* should not be too brown, but creamy-beige in colour. I keep rolling the rest of the *nechis* between bouts of frying. Hot *luchis* should never be covered, or they will go limp.

Though you can eat *luchis* with almost anything, even by themselves, on the evening of Ashtami they would always be served with two classic vegetarian dishes associated with ceremonial occasions: a potato dish called *alur dam* and a *dal* made with yellow split peas and tiny pieces of coconut. There are many variations of the *alur dam*, but usually on Ashtami this light version, flavoured with a pinch of asafoetida, was made in our house. A *dam* usually means something cooked while covered for a long time over a low heat. However, potatoes do not have to be cooked for a very long time. *Alur dam*, has, in Bengali, come to mean a dish of potatoes, usually whole or quartered, coated in a thick spicy sauce. It is usually eaten with *luchis* or wheat-flour chapatis, not rice.

 To make **Alur dam** for four to five people, take 500 g (1 lb) potatoes. Boil and peel them – in that order – and quarter them. Take 3–4 dry red chillies and 3–4 teaspoons of whole cumin seeds. Toast them in a dry frying pan over a medium flame until the chillies are dark brown. Remove and grind them as fine as you can in a pestle or on a grinding stone. (If, however, this seems too much trouble, take 3–4 teaspoons each of cumin and chilli powder and toast them together in a frying pan. The taste and flavour will be pretty good, though not as good as that of freshly ground spices.) Next, take 1½ teaspoons of tamarind extract and mix it smoothly in a bowl with 60 ml (2 fl oz) of hot water. Set aside. Heat 3 tablespoons of mustard oil in a *karai* and throw in 2–3 bay leaves, 1 teaspoon of *panch phoron* and a tiny pinch or ⅛ teaspoon of asafoetida crumbled between your fingers. As the *panch*

phoron stops sputtering, put in the potatoes and sprinkle over them ¼ teaspoon of turmeric powder. Stir repeatedly until they turn golden brown and pour in 400 ml (13 fl oz) of water. Once it comes to the boil, reduce the heat to medium and simmer for four to five minutes. Then add salt to taste, 2 teaspoons of the roasted spices and the tamarind paste. Stir thoroughly for another three to four minutes and taste to find your balance of salt and sour. You can add more or less of the roasted powder depending on your tolerance for hot food. If the gravy becomes too thick, or too sour, more water can be added.

The *dal* that was served together with this was a little more laborious. In the days before the pressure cooker it was a pain to cook, for these yellow split peas could take more than half a day to get done, but now most middle-class families, even those with working women, can easily serve this kind of *dal* by using a pressure cooker.

For **Chholar dal** to feed four people, my mother would weigh out 250 g (½ lb) of yellow split peas and cook them in the pressure cooker with double the amount of water, 3 bay leaves and 3 whole red chillies. She left the cooker for about fifteen to twenty minutes on a high flame. By then the cooked *dal* would be of a thickish consistency and the individual grains would be soft but unbroken. This she would empty out in a bowl and set aside. Then she would take one half of a whole coconut and pry out half the flesh from the shell. The brown skin at the back would be painstakingly peeled with a sharp knife. If you find this too hard, you can try soaking the coconut for ten minutes in a bowl of hot water. Once peeled, the coconut would be chopped into tiny pieces and fried in 2 tablespoons of sizzling mustard oil in a large *karai* until they turned pink. She would add 1½ teaspoons of whole cumin seeds to the coconut and fry them for a couple of minutes before adding ½ teaspoon of ginger paste, ½ teaspoon of ground chilli, 1 teaspoon each of fresh ground cumin and coriander and salt to taste. Once all this had been fried for two to three minutes, she would pour the *dal* into the *karai*. (On bad days when there were no freshly ground spices and she had to fall back on powdered spices, she would pour in the *dal* after frying the coconut and the whole cumin, adding the other spices later.) The *dal* would be checked for salt, 400 ml (13 fl oz) of water added and the whole mixture assiduously stirred until the grains were smashed. Some sugar, about 3 teaspoons, would be added; this is a *dal* in which the sweetness should be a little pronounced. Just before removing the *dal* from the fire, she would add 1 tablespoon of ghee and 2 teaspoons of ground *garom mashla*.

To finish off the Ashtami dinner, there was usually the simplest of desserts, *kheer*, of which we never tired. This was simply milk, evaporated slowly over a low flame. Though it must originally have started as a measure to preserve and utilise excess milk in the days before refrigeration, *kheer* remains a great favourite in Bengali households. When made as a chosen dessert, one l (1¾ pints) of milk, reduced to about 600 ml (1 pint), was considered to be of the right consistency. Once that was done, sugar, the amount varying according to the cook's preference, would be added and the pan removed from the stove and left to cool. Sometimes tangerines from the rare first crop, an expensive treat, would be peeled and the inner pulp from the segments stirred into the cool *kheer*. If it is added before the *kheer* has cooled, the acid in the tangerine can cut the milk and destroy the thick, creamy texture of the *kheer*. Mop this up with *luchis* or eat in sensuous spoonfuls and you will come very close to absolute bliss.

Navami, the last day of Durga's stay, is gastronomically the opposite of Ashtami; meat-eating is the order of the day. This practice dates from the time-honoured custom of offering live sacrifices of goats and buffaloes to the goddess and eating the holy sacrificial meat the same day. The priest who killed the animals had to be a strong man, for ritual demanded the severing of head and body with one blow. Failure on the part of the priest was looked upon as an ominous sign that the goddess was displeased and refused to accept the sacrifice. The meat would then be cooked following special recipes without any onion or garlic, which were regarded by the Hindus as heathen ingredients.

The huge courtyards in the houses of the wealthy where the sacrifice was made must have been a gory sight. If goats were the offering, as was most often the case, several would be slaughtered one after the other and the entire courtyard would reek of blood. There are gruesome stories of nineteenth-century Calcutta where young men would hold wrestling matches on the bloody courtyards in the afternoon. Each time they fell they would be covered with the sacrificial blood and slime until they all looked like the figures in a nightmare. Finally, as the evening fell, these bloody apparitions would set out with torches and march triumphantly through the neighbouring streets.

Today no community *puja* will organise the sacrifice of animals and the meat eaten on Navami is, except in a very few houses, bought from the markets as on any other day. For those who do not wish to sacrifice animals, vegetables like pumpkins, gourds and coconuts are used as substitutes. This is probably due to the influence of the Vaishnavs who abhor violence and must also be linked to the increasing economic difficulty of buying sacrificial animals. As a result, the terrifying and trauma-ridden ceremony of sacrifice has been reduced almost to a comedy in which the earnest priest has to decorate the sacrificial pumpkin with the obligatory vermilion, turmeric and oil and split it with one blow of the knife. The one thing that remains from the old days is Navami meat, often cooked without onion or garlic. In our house, my parents did not avoid those ingredients, but my grandmother, before she was widowed, always cooked her meat without these heathen alliums. Instead of the heavy, almost oppressive aroma of onion and garlic, her cooking filled the house with a delicate flavour of cumin and coriander. After all these years and the taste of so many meat preparations, I can still recall the taste of the Navami meat of my childhood. On rare occasions my mother, whose sense of nostalgia is even stronger than mine, still cooks meat her mother's way. When trying this recipe, you might need to add more water or cook the meat longer, depending on its quality.

 We have always called this dish **Grandmother's meat without onion and garlic**. At home it would be made with goat meat, but lamb can be easily substituted. The front leg or lamb chops can provide suitable meat. My mother takes 500 g (1 lb) meat, cuts it into small cubes, rinses it in cold water and mixes it with 60 g (2 oz) of yoghurt, 3 teaspoons of turmeric, a little salt and 1 tablespoon of mustard oil. This marinaded meat is left covered at room temperature for an hour. Meanwhile, she organises her spices. *Garom mashla*, consisting of 2 cardamoms, 4 cloves and 2 pieces of cinnamon, 2.5 cm (1 in) long, is ground with water. Apart from this she needs 6 teaspoons each of freshly ground cumin and coriander, 4 teaspoons of ground ginger, 4 teaspoons of ground mustard and 2 teaspoons (you can use less) of ground red chillies. Some days I have seen her add 4–5 teaspoons of ground *posto* as well. Once the meat was marinaded, she would heat 60 ml (2 fl oz) of oil in a thick-bottomed pan and throw in 3–4 bay leaves. As they turned brown, she would add the meat with its marinade. This would be stirred for three to four minutes, covered and left on a medium flame. Within five to six minutes a lot of moisture would be generated and she would add all the ground spices except the *garom mashla*. Then the meat would be stirred vigorously until all the moisture evaporated and it almost started sticking to the bottom of the pan. Often good meat can become quite tender by this time. She would add 500 ml (16 fl oz) of hot water for the gravy, like sauce, and leave the meat on the stove until it was absolutely tender. Finally, she would heat

2 teaspoons of oil in a small saucepan and blend the *garom mashla* in it. This would be added to the meat, the pot left tightly covered until mealtime so that none of the fragrance escaped. Some years this would be served with *luchis*, other years with rice.

Though I have never seen animals being sacrificed to the goddess, I have witnessed a religious festival where sacrificial blood and meat are pivotal elements. This is the great Muslim festival of Id-uz-Zoha or Bakr-id, observed in commemoration of the prophet Abraham's willingness to sacrifice his son in devotion to the Lord. Cows and *khashis*, castrated goats, are fattened before being brought to the market and bought by the devout according to their means. Cows being expensive, it is only the wealthy who can afford to offer one. Sometimes several families pool their resources to buy one.

The first time I witnessed the ceremony in Dhaka, Bakr-id happened to fall in the winter and by the end of the day I was very glad it was cold. We happened to live in an affluent residential area and almost every family around us offered animals for sacrifice. By mid-afternoon, the stream of blood from our wealthy landlord's offering of one cow and two *khashis* had almost covered the front entrance. Hordes of beggars were besieging every gate because Islam demands that you donate a portion of your sacrificial or *korbani* meat to them.

Since the amount of *korbani* meat left, even after distribution, is too much to consume at one time, Bengali Muslims have devised a way of cooking the extra meat, especially beef, with onion, garlic, ginger, salt, bay leaf and oil. When the meat is half-cooked, some *garom mashla* is added. Heated once every day in the summer and on alternate days in the winter, this meat keeps quite well for a month. Towards the end, the repeated heating tends to make some of the meat flaky, but the unique taste, produced by the very slow cooking, proves that making a virtue of necessity is not as bad as it sounds.

The three days of Durga Puja are over only too soon and
the last day, Bijoya Dashami, the tenth of the new moon,
finds everyone preparing to say farewell to the goddess and
her children. The daughter has to leave her indulgent home
and go back to the reality of life with her ascetic husband.
The married women of each neighbourhood go to the
pandals to offer *sindur*, the vermilion powder they wear as a
red mark on the parting in their hair and on their foreheads.
They smear it on the forehead of the goddess and her feet and
then on each other's foreheads and partings to protect
themselves from the misfortune of widowhood.

I once happened to have lunch on this day with a very
traditional East Bengali family and they served an *ambal*
made with *shapla*, the stalks of water lilies, a dish that I have
never seen elsewhere. The elderly mother told me that in the
old days this would be offered to the goddess together with
fermented rice soaked overnight in water. Both these items,
inexpensive and easily available in any rural household, were
primarily eaten by women who not only enjoyed their tangy
flavour but also ate them to save more of the 'important'
items like fresh rice, fish or meat or milk for the men. The fact
that the goddess is offered such humble items along with
expensive fruits, milk-based sweets and sacrificial meat is an
indication of how much the women of Bengal have identified
themselves with her. The distance between deity and devotee
disappears in the closeness between mother and daughter, in
the bond between woman and woman.

On the evening of Bijoya Dashami, the images in the
community *pandals* are loaded on to trucks and taken to the
nearest river for the final rite of *bhashan*, throwing them into
the water. It is then, in the wake of the departed goddess, that
the most beautiful aspect of Bijoya Dashami comes – the
discarding of all ill-feelings of hostility, anger and envy.
Within the family, younger people touch their elders' feet in
pronam and receive their blessings, while contemporaries
embrace each other with good wishes. As the evening
deepens, relatives, friends and neighbours drop in to convey

their Bijoya greetings. They must be offered sweets, which cannot be refused – I have even seen diabetics put fragments into their mouths to honour the custom. And so the visits go on until the day of the full moon, the visitors bringing along more sweets to add to the household stock. The commonest sweet is the *sandesh*, because it is dry and easy to carry. But there is nothing to stop you from bringing an earthen pot of *rosogollas* swimming in syrup, or even variations like *rajbhog* or *pantua*. None of these are made at home, for most people do not wish to rival the *moira*, the professional sweet-maker.

Some years, when my mother happened to be in the mood, she would spend part of her Bijoya afternoon making two home-made sweets which were a refreshing change from the cloying commercial products that would flood our house at that time.

One of them was the **Patishapta**, a delicious Bengali variant of sweet, stuffed crêpes. With a bit of practice, it becomes one of the easiest of desserts. First she would make the filling. She would grind the flesh extracted from one half of a good large coconut on a special coconut grinder and mix it with 250 g (8 oz) of brown sugar, *gur*, or if that was not to hand, white sugar. The mixture would be cooked in a *karai* over a medium flame. Usually a separate *karai* is used for sweet preparations, so that none of the strong lingering smells of spices can invade the delicate flavour of sweets and milk. After ten to twelve minutes of constant stirring, the sugar and the coconut would be evenly blended and a lovely caramelised smell would fill the air. Sometimes she would need to add more sugar, and if it was white, she would also grind 2 whole cardamoms and add them to the coconut mixture at this stage. As soon as it was cool enough to touch, she would divide it into twelve to thirteen portions, shaping each into a roll about 10 cm (4 in) long. These would be covered and set aside.

To make the crêpes, she would take 250 g (½ lb) of flour and mix it thoroughly with 2 tablespoons of peanut oil or ghee. If they were not to be eaten immediately, she would use a mixture of flour and cream of wheat to keep the crêpes soft. Then she would add 250 ml (8 fl oz) of water and 2 tablespoons of sugar and mix it carefully to form a liquid thick enough to roll over the surface of a tilted frying pan. When she was satisfied with the consistency, she would take the medium-sized frying pan, heat it slightly and grease it carefully with peanut oil. In Bengal the usual way to do this is by taking the discarded stem of an aubergine and rubbing the pan with the flat end that was attached to the aubergine. The important thing is not to add too much oil. The pan would then be put over a medium flame, a large serving spoon or a cooking ladle full of the liquid poured in, and the pan tilted to spread the liquid evenly. As soon as the batter started cooking into a golden skin, she would wedge a spatula under the surface to loosen it from the pan. Then she would take one of the coconut rolls, place it close to one edge of the crêpe and roll the two together like a stuffed mat. Pressing down on the *patishapta* gently with her spatula, she would flip it over until both sides were brown, remove it from the pan and start on the next crêpe, greasing the pan carefully. When this was being served as a dessert for special guests, my mother would go one step further. She would evaporate some milk to make a thick *kheer*. Some chopped almonds would be cooked in this *kheer* and a flavouring of ground cardamom would be added. Then it would be poured over the waiting *patishaptas*, much as chocolate sauce is poured over desserts in the West.

The other home-made sweet that appeared on Bijoya Dashami, this one primarily for my benefit, was the *malpo*, flat, round fennel-seed dumplings in syrup. This is quite simple to make and appears often in our house.

To make **Malpo**, first the syrup has to be prepared. The consistency is important, for if it is too thin the *malpos* tend to fall apart. I find that 250 g (8 oz) of sugar with 5 tablespoons of water and a teaspoon of lemon juice is about right. Once the syrup has boiled, my mother sets it aside. Then she mixes 250 g (8 oz) of flour with 2 tablespoons of peanut oil and when they are blended smoothly, adds 250 ml (8 fl oz) of whole milk and a teaspoon of whole fennel seeds. These give the *malpos* their distinctive taste. Then she heats about 120 ml (4 fl oz) of oil in her *karai*, lowers the flame to medium and, taking large spoonfuls of the flour mixture, drops them in, one at a time. Each round *malpo* is fried carefully until both sides are brown and the edges curl up crisply. Nothing can be worse than half-done *malpos*. Once all of them are fried, she dips them in the syrup, turns them over and lays them out on a flat serving dish. Then the rest of the syrup is poured over them. These keep well without losing their taste − there is nothing like the surreptitious pleasure of quickly eating a *malpo* in the middle of your day's work when you are sure nobody is looking.

Durga's departure is hardly over before it is time for Lakshmi, her daughter, goddess of wealth and prosperity, to arrive. Though much removed from their past lives in the villages, urban settlers have not forgotten what they owe to this prim golden goddess. Durga might deliver you from crises and unforeseen dangers, but without Lakshmi's blessings the wherewithals of life would be sadly lacking. Women, particularly, are her devotees, and daughters and wives are often referred to as the Lakshmi of the home. Their beauty, or grace, too, is attributed to her generosity. So it is that her seat is right in the centre of every good Hindu home. Each family, whether rich or poor, has its own little niche where a picture or image of Lakshmi is ensconced to be worshipped by women every Thursday. Symbolically, a basket decorated with cowries, which were used as currency at one time, is kept by the image.

It is on the autumn full moon that Lakshmi is worshipped with special rites and ceremony. One popular song eulogises the state of grace the world has achieved because of her blessings: the rivers are full of gently burbling waters that reflect the stars in the sky, the fields are full of golden grain and each household has one or more of the plump brown cows whose copious flow of milk is like a tidal wave of white flowers. Perhaps it is this association of milk with plenitude that makes *payesh*, or Bengali rice pudding, one of the most important offerings for Lakshmi in Bengali homes.

But in Bengal wealth and prosperity are not easy to come by, and Lakshmi demands more than rituals, offerings and compliments from her followers. The autumn full moon is called *kojagori* and thereby hangs a tale. The word is derived from the Sanskrit *ko jagarti*, meaning 'who's awake?' Legend says that on this night the goddess flies all over the earth, carried on the back of her faithful white owl, asking who is awake. Those who can fight lethargy and stay up are the beneficiaries of the goddess's good graces for the coming year. And while you stay up, you have to play dice with your spouse – the game being particularly appropriate for the occasion, for the goddess is almost as fickle in her favours as the dice. In their eagerness to hold her to their homes, Bengali women paint outlines of her little feet on their floors in a line from the front door to where the image of the goddess has been placed, as if she has just walked in and gone and sat down in her niche. Fancifully, they believe that if the footprints are only depicted going into the house, then she will be unable to leave.

Payesh, made in Lakshmi's honour is always distributed among neighbours or relatives. It is usually cooked outside the kitchen in specially sanctified surroundings. Usually a portable stove and special pots and utensils are used. Our *payesh*, very different from the insipid, somewhat glutinous dish that is served in institutional kitchens in the West, is derived from the Sanskrit word *paramanno*, which means the ultimate or best kind of rice. With time, of course, the ingenious Bengali has devised many kinds of *payesh* that do not have any rice, but one fundamental rule remains: *payesh* is something that has to be cooked in milk, and there are no short cuts like using any kind of canned, evaporated or condensed milk. For the very special taste of *payesh* (as of *kheer*) comes from the milk being very slowly reduced in volume over a low flame. Cream, which is such an important ingredient in the West, is hardly used in Bengal, probably because the tropical climate makes it difficult to skim the cream from the milk. And cold or chilled milk is never drunk, it is always boiled to kill the bacteria. However when hot milk is left uncovered, a thick skin will form and that is often skimmed off to be heated over low temperatures and yield ghee. In *payesh* the sweetening agent is usually plain sugar, except in the winter when date-palm sap is available and lends its own distinctive flavour to the milk. Brown sugar from sugar-cane is never used because it tends to ruin the creamy texture of evaporated milk.

In our family the rice used for *payesh* is usually one of the small-grained fragrant varieties like Gobindabhog. When that is not available, Basmati is the next best option. *Payesh* can be served either at room temperature or chilled, but it tends to thicken as it gets colder. Personally, I find a little goes a long way since it is so rich, but some people can gobble up enormous helpings.

To make **Payesh** for four to six people, take about 75 g (2½ oz) of Basmati rice, rinse it in a colander and spread it out on a tray to dry. Mix it thoroughly with 2 teaspoons of ghee. This will prevent it from becoming sticky and forming lumps when it is being cooked in the milk. Set aside the rice. Take 2 l (3½ pints) of whole milk in a deep, thick-bottomed pan. This, like the *karai* for *patishapta*, has to be uncontaminated by spices; in Bengali homes a couple of pots are usually set aside for boiling the milk and to cook *kheer* or *payesh*. Bring the milk to a boil over a high heat and immediately reduce to a low flame. Now comes the painstaking part of evaporating it, stirring constantly so that it does not stick to the bottom of the pan or boil over. After about an hour, or when the milk has been reduced to about 1.5 l (2½ pints) add the rice and keep stirring until it is cooked. You need to check the grains repeatedly, otherwise the rice will become a mush. If the milk is absorbed too fast, you can add a little more. Once the rice has been cooked, start adding sugar. Pour in 120 g (4 oz), then keep adding until you reach the sweetness you wish. Some of my friends prefer very sweet *payesh*, but I find it too cloying. If you wish to add almonds and pistachios for garnishing, they will have to be soaked in a bowl of hot water to soften them, as hard nuts are not acceptable in Bengali food. Peel and chop the soaked nuts before you start on the *payesh*. Throw them in at the end and cook for a couple of minutes. You can also add a heaped tablespoon of raisins to this. Finally, grind 2–3 whole cardamoms and add for flavouring before removing from the heat. If you do not like cardamoms you can add a little *keora* water (sold bottled in Indian grocery stores) once the *payesh* has cooled. Or you can put 3 pieces of cinnamon, 2.5 cm (1 in) long, into the milk as it evaporates. Make sure to throw them out before serving.

Two weeks after the worship of Lakshmi, on the dark night of the new moon, Bengal invokes the terrible Kali, dark goddess of power. Naked, ornamented only with a necklace of skulls and a skirt made of severed human arms, she is the black side of Durga, the destructive fury who can rage through all creation unconscious of the havoc she wreaks. In her rampaging fury, she has stepped on her husband Shiva, the detached ascetic, which has finally brought her to her senses – we see her biting her tongue in shame.

The devotees of Kali are supposed to drink some kind of alcohol, usually brewed from rice (often referred to as *karan bari*), on this night, but that practice is no longer much in evidence. Drinking is not really part of the traditional Bengali's life. There are, however, many hilarious stories of the feudal days when Kali was worshipped at home by wealthy people, particularly those of the Shakto sect, especially those or who considered themselves Tantrics. As the night progressed, master and servant would lose all sense of respective status because of the unusual quantities of alcohol in the system. The servant could be seen ordering his master about and the latter busily trying to carry out those orders, but unable to do so because he could not even walk straight!

The only observance in our house was on the eve of Kali Puja. Since that is the fourteenth day after the full moon and since Kali is supposed to be attended by fourteen demonic attendants, the number fourteen assumes mystical significance. Fourteen dots of vermilion and oil paste are painted on the walls of the house to protect the inhabitants from the supernatural forces. And fourteen varieties of leafy greens (small samples, tied together, are sold in the markets) have to be eaten with rice at lunch. In the evening fourteen candles or oil lamps are lit and placed on window seats and balconies.

By the end of the month of Kartik, the first month of Hemanta or late autumn, urban Bengalis resume the normal pattern of life in school, college and office. In rural Bengal, however, this is a time of great expectations, for the following month, Agrahayan, is also the time to harvest the rice that gave the region its sobriquet 'golden Bengal' in the first line of the national anthem of Bangladesh. The name itself, *Agrahayan*, is compounded of two words – *agra*, best or foremost, and *hayan* or unhusked rice. Many scholars believe this was originally the first month of the Bengali calendar, not only because it would be natural for ordinary farming people to calculate a year around major agricultural events, but also because Agrahayan is considered the best of all months for weddings. Of course, this is partly a practical matter; the mellow temperatures make the rich food for the guests and the heavy brocaded silks and jewellery for the bride more bearable. But for Bengalis there is a special aura of auspiciousness about the first month of the year. For the second most important month for Bengali weddings is Baisakh, the current first calendar month when the heat of the summer is on full blast.

In the countryside, Agrahayan is a time of hard work. In good years, when the monsoon has been just right, the fields are full of the standing rice crop that needs to be harvested and brought home. Most of that is still done by hand, as it has been for centuries. Under the bearable autumn sun, the peasants cut the rice with their sickles and tie it in golden bunches to be transported by bullock carts. Slowly, as the days progress, the once golden fields become stretches of stubble, the dead remnants of the plant being gathered later for animal feed and supplementary fuel. In the evenings, as the first chill of oncoming winter is felt, some of the rice straw is used for small fires in front of which people can sit and warm themselves. Once the rice has been harvested and stored in woven straw-covered bins, the work of threshing, husking and milling begins. Women help with the threshing, beating the bunches of harvested crop against the beaten earth floors of village courtyards. Rice which will be parboiled is cooked in the husk in huge vats of water and set out to dry in the sun before being taken to the nearest mills.

In the old days, before mills or any kind of technology, it was the women who did the back-breaking job of husking the rice. The traditional Bengali instrument for taking the husk off the rice is called a *dhenki*, a long wooden board mounted on a short pedestal in the middle, much like a see-saw. One end of the board has a short pestle-like attachment underneath and that is positioned over a large shallow depression in the ground where the unhusked rice is kept. It requires two women to handle the *dhenki*. One stands near the end without the pestle and presses it down with her foot. As soon as she releases her foot, the board dips down to the other end, the pestle hitting the rice with force, thus separating the husk from the grain. As she presses with her foot and lifts the board from the rice, the other woman turns the rice over with her hand, so that all the grains can be hit evenly. It is an infinitely time-consuming process, and is no longer viable, but some food aficionados claim that rice husked by a *dhenki* is far superior in taste to rice processed in a mill. This may be because the *dhenki* always leaves some of the inner husk on the grain, whether parboiled or *atap*, thus making it more nutritious. The long hours of monotonous labour with the *dhenki* have made the word a symbol for unquestioning drudgery. A Bengali proverb says that even if a *dhenki* is transported to heaven, it will find some rice to husk.

In the unlucky years, of course, this happy intensity of work is less visible. Sometimes the late autumn comes with the most disastrous rainstorms and vicious cyclones. Agrahayan, then, is a time of despair. Apart from destroying the rural settlements and killing human beings and livestock, these angry visitations can also decimate fields of standing rice. In Bengal we have a whole body of sayings supposed to have come down from the legendary wise woman, Khana, daughter-in-law of the equally legendary scholar/astrologer, Barahamihir. Most of these sayings are centred around the weather, cropping patterns and different aspects of rural life. It is said that so correct were Khana's pronouncements that her father-in-law cut off her tongue in a fit of male jealousy. But well before she was silenced, Khana had made her prediction: if it rains in Agrahayan, even the king will have to go begging. The fields of Agrahayan are not then acres of golden bounty but a miserable expanse of underdeveloped or rotting crops.

Aside from expending energy in garnering and processing the Aman rice, some Bengali peasants also start working on their winter crops, or preparing the land for them. In areas where the date-palm tree is plentiful, late autumn is the time to start tapping the juice from the trunks. This juice or sap, called *khejur ras*, is one of the most delightful gifts of nature, like maple syrup in North America. The first few tappings do not provide the best juice, though the pale and fragrant liquid can be a refreshing morning drink, but later tappings through the winter produce a rich, thick liquid, which is slowly boiled to make various kinds of *gur* liquid, grainy liquid or solid. The wonderful fragrance of *gur* on the fire spreads far and wide, and is one of the most pleasing aspects of Bengali rural life in autumn and winter.

For rural Hindu women, and even their urban counterparts as late as the 1950s, Agrahayan was also the month for a quaint ritual in honour of the sun called Ritu or Itu Puja. My mother and all her younger sisters who were born and raised in Calcutta observed this ritual with great regularity until they were married, and there were some attempts to induct me into this practice too. Entirely feminine, it combines beautifully women's awareness of nature and a celebration of fertility. On the last day of Kartik (the month preceding Agrahayan), a large open-mouthed earthen pot, *malsha*, would be filled with moist earth and five kinds of grain, including rice, would be scattered over the top. A little pitcher, usually copper, would then be filled with water and set firmly into the mound of earth. The women would fast, bathe and chant the relevant *mantras*, make an offering of seasonal fruit, and water the earth in the pot. Then one of them would tell a well-known story about the Sun-god. Finally, the earthen pot would be placed in a special corner of the house. As the days of the month went by, the seeds in the pot would germinate into sprouts and long green leaves. Every Sunday – Rabibar, the day of the sun in Bengali – the ritual of fasting, chanting, watering and story-telling would be repeated. By the end of the month, some, if not all, of the rice in the field had been harvested and brought home. So, on the final day of Agrahayan, the Sun-god would receive a final offering of rice pudding made with the new rice and sweetened with the earliest *gur*. After this, the whole pot would be immersed in the nearest pond, water tank or river.

Once the rice has been harvested, rural Bengal propitiates the gods for their bounty through the joyful festival of *nabanno*, which literally means 'new rice'. Radha Prasad Gupta, a chronicler of many aspects of Bengali life, once recounted to me his childhood memories of *nabanno* with something close to ecstasy. The mingled fragrance of the uncooked offering for the gods – a combination of milk, *gur*, pieces of sugar-cane, bananas, and above all, the new rice – was unique enough to linger in his memory throughout his life. Even in Bangladesh, where the majority of the people are Muslims and do not have the Hindu pantheon to propitiate, some cultural commonality can be seen in the celebration of the new rice. Once the gods have received their dues, the new rice and the season's first *gur* are cooked in milk to make a *payesh* which has to be distributed among the neighbours. Rich farmers are obviously in a position to be more punctilious and generous in this respect than landless peasants and sharecroppers.

Unlike the summer in the West, autumn, early or late depending on the Puja holidays, is the time when urban Bengalis take their holidays. Schools and colleges are closed for a month or so and the weather is ideal for travelling within Bengal or to any other part of India except the northernmost areas. After the establishment of an extensive and efficient railway system by the British, train travel *en famille* during the autumn holidays became an institution. Despite the presence of dining cars, the best part of these journeys usually consisted of opening up your 'tiffin carrier' and consuming the *luchis*, *alur dam*, dry curried meat and the *mishtis* you had brought from home.

The tranquil fullness of nature in the autumn also imbues the waters of Bengal and rural people can sometimes indulge themselves with amateur fishing, spending contemplative afternoons with bait and line. There is a wonderful variety of fish to choose from. Iswarchandra Gupta, the nineteenth-century Bengali poet who in his writing glorified food with eulogy, mischief, humour and ecstasy, used one of them to celebrate the fish found in autumn: small fish like punti, mourala, tangra and bele, the round-bellied pomfret, the pankal, baan and gule of the eel family, shingi and magur of the catfish family, estuarine delectables like parshe, bhetki, bhangar and, of course, the earliest specimens of king prawn, the galda chingri.

Many of these fish are cooked with strong, pungent sauces because they themselves have strong flavours and very firm flesh. The eel-like creatures have the advantage of having no bones apart from the spine. Nor do they have any scales, so they can be easily cut up into 5–8 cm (2–3 in) pieces and cooked with a ground mustard sauce like the hilsa during the monsoon, or just a fiery red chilli sauce. Green chillies are added for extra zest and the *phoron* is either *kalo jeera* or *panch phoron*. The magur and the bhetki are treated differently. They are more expensive and are generally bought for guests or on special occasions. Magur, quite apart from its taste, has the distinction of working wonders on the invalid's system, if plainly cooked. And if you are not an invalid, what more wonderful than a *kalia* made of magur, the rich dark gravy spiced with freshly ground cumin, coriander, ginger, turmeric, red chilli and *garom mashla*? Bhetki, can be made into a *kalia* too, but I tend to prefer it more lightly cooked with chopped garlic, ground mustard and green chillies. The British in Bengal doted on this fish because it was boneless and could easily be cut into fillets to be cooked in a Western style and also, perhaps because the flavour reminded them of fish at home. The years of cohabitation also taught the wily Bengali the potential of bhetki. Even the word fillet has become part of the Bengali language, with the final 't' well pronounced. At weddings and other formal occasions, these fillets of bhetki are made into 'fries', another instance of the adoption of a foreign word. The fillets are marinaded in an onion, ginger and red chilli paste to which salt and lemon juice have been added. They are then dipped in egg, coated with breadcrumbs and deep-fried in oil. Those who like fish and chips can try this variant.

Of course such anglicised preparations are mostly urban. Small towns and villages, even in the early part of this century, were quite innocent of elaborate culinary practices based on the food of the ruling race. My father spent several years during his boyhood at a residential school in Bankura district in northern West Bengal, a quiet provincial place where the only technology was probably the presence of the railway. Here even ordinary things like biscuits or commercially-baked loaves of bread were unknown before the Second World War. Instead, the standard breakfast fare during the autumn season was a clutch of homely *bhabras*, hot crispy fritters, made from *besan* or chick-pea flour, mixed with water, salt, ground chilli and a little rice flour for crispness. The thick batter was left overnight in the kitchen to ferment a little, and in the morning the cook would heat a lot of oil in his large *karai*. Then he would take some of the fermented mixture and put it in a bit of cloth with a small hole in it. Holding the cloth bundle over the hot oil, he would squeeze the mixture out through the hole to form separate collections of concentric circles. The crisp, hot fritters would be gobbled up with great relish by the hungry hordes that sat waiting. For those schoolboys, the famous Calcutta bakeries, Firpo's – now closed – and Flury's, were as unimaginable as the fancy pastries and loaves they sold. All over the north-western districts of West Bengal, Bankura, Birbhum and Puruliya, these homely *bhabras* were common breakfast items. Now, however, even the most god-forsaken village will have a teashop selling biscuits and buns.

In the countryside Agrahayan is also the traditional month for making *boris*, little pellets made from *dal* soaked in water, ground to a fine paste on the grinding stone and then dried in the sun. Salt and appropriate spices are added to the paste. The white *kalai dal* (sold as *urat dal* in most Indian grocery stores abroad), for instance, is often flavoured with ground asafoetida. Once the *dal* paste is spiced, a clean cloth is spread out on a large plate or tray, little blobs of the paste placed on it in rows and left to dry in the sun for several days until all the moisture has evaporated. Once thoroughly dried, the *boris* are packed in large tins and stored for the coming year.

Bori-making has always been an exclusively feminine art, traditionally associated with elderly women, widowed grandmothers and aunts. One of the reasons was perhaps that such women had already reached menopause and were free of the 'unclean' days of the month during which younger women were not supposed to do anything requiring cleanliness or purity. Bengali literature abounds with references to a whole army of cosy older women turning out *boris*. Many rituals grew up around this domestic duty. Even if a young married woman set out to make *boris*, she would first bathe and purify herself. Once she had the paste ready, she would take a portion and shape them into two huge *boris*, called *buro* and *buri*, old man and old woman. These would be crowned with unhusked rice paddy and *durba* grass (a part of any *puja* ritual from ancient times) and the woman would pray to them for the success of her *bori*-making.

As with all art, the *boris* reflected the hand that made them. The consistency of the *dal*, the degree of spicing and the intensity of whipping the paste before making the pellets all varied from woman to woman. *Kalai dal*, for instance, is used to make a variety called *phulboris*, which are feather-light and melt in the mouth once fried in oil. The woman who could whip the *dal* hard enough to make the lightest *phulboris* acquired a reputation. In one famous novel, *Arogyaniketan*, a character is even identified by the memory of the *phulboris* made by his grandmother.

By now, of course, much of the mystique of *bori*-making is over. They are made commercially on a large scale and dried in ovens. Even in our home, which is very traditional, *boris* have never been home-made. Nor are commercial *boris* ritually made in Agrahayan. Inevitably, mass production means some diminution in quality, but the great advantage is that packaged *boris* are now available in Indian grocery stores around the world. The larger ones are fried and used in fish or vegetable stews, while the smaller ones, fried crisper, are crumbled over cooked leafy greens as well as other vegetables. Being made of *dal*, they served as a welcome optional source of protein for widows and other vegetarians. One of my most favourite applications of *bori* is slightly unorthodox. But it is very easy to make anywhere and lends an extra dimension to a Bengali classic, *begun pora*, or spiced roasted aubergine.

Select big, round, fat purple aubergines for **Begun pora** – the rounder they are, the better. Usually 2 large ones are enough for four people. Cut each one into four sections, but leave them joined near the stem. Now rub some oil on the outer surfaces of the aubergines. The best way to make *begun pora* is to roast them over a gas flame. In the absence of a gas stove, heat the oven to 230°C (450°F, gas mark 8), place the aubergines on a foil-covered baking dish and roast them evenly on all sides. They will have to be turned around several times until the skin turns completely black and peels off easily. Some of the juices will run out on the foil. Check if the flesh is cooked by inserting a fork into the portion closest to the stem, which is the firmest and takes longest to cook. If they are roasted directly on a flame, as is the tradition in Bengal, the outer skin is charred to a crisp and falls off in crackling pieces. The final product also tastes better, but it also makes a mess to be cleaned up. When the aubergines are done, take them out and let them cool. Meanwhile, take a handful of small *boris* and fry them in oil over a high heat until they are very brown. Take 1 small onion and chop it as fine as possible. Then chop 1–2 green chillies and 1 small handful of coriander leaves. By this time the aubergines should be cool. Peel off the blackened skin carefully. If they have been done in an oven, the skin will not be so crisp and will come off with some of the flesh adhering to it. Scrape the flesh away with a spoon before discarding the skin. Dipping your hands in a bowl of cold water helps when you are peeling the skin. Cut off the stems, mash the flesh thoroughly with a fork and mix in the chopped onion, chilli and coriander together with salt to taste and 4–5 teaspoons of pungent mustard oil. Crumble the *boris* and add them to the mixture. This tastes equally good with rice or chapatis or even by itself. Like the Middle Eastern *baba ganoush*, it can also be served as an appetiser, with small bits of unleavened bread.

As the autumn ripens to its own fullness, the days shorten, the twilight lessens and intimations of mortality whisper in the smoky evening air, I always feel a subdued melancholy.

Perhaps this is because both my grandfathers died in the autumn, one early and one late, in successive years, and death among the Hindus, like birth and marriage, has a protracted set of rituals which surround one with their oppressive presence.

Thankfully, being a grandchild, I was spared the sight of the crematorium and the funeral pyre. Only the sons of the dead have to be present at the cremation, which usually takes place near a river. Once the body is reduced to ashes, the mourners bathe in the river, don new *dhotis* (worn from the waist down) and cover their upper bodies with a *chadar* or light shawl. Stitched clothing is absolutely forbidden and mourning women are supposed to wear their saris without blouses. Once they have bathed, a small piece of iron (a key, for instance) is strung round the neck of each mourner. This is supposed to act like a barrier and protect the living from the dead.

The period of mourning varies. In our family it lasted eleven days because we were Brahmins. Other castes have lesser restrictions. During all this time my uncles and their wives had to wear their unstitched clothes, walk barefoot and sleep on the floor on a blanket. The men could not shave and neither men nor women could oil or comb their hair. The absence of oil extended to food also. Cooking was permissible only at lunchtime when rice and green bananas would be boiled in an earthen pot over a wood fire to make the prescribed *habishanno*. The only seasoning the mourners could use was ghee and a bit of coarsely ground sea salt. Once in a while, a bit of ground *dal* would be thrown into the pot of rice to make it more nutritious. Dinner invariably consisted of fruit and milk.

On the tenth day my uncles went for a ritual bath in the Ganga and threw away the iron round their necks. Afterwards another set of clothes, unstitched again, was given to them. The old ones were given to the barber waiting there to trim their nails and shave their beards and heads. Women only have their nails trimmed.

On the morning of the eleventh day the priest conducted the *shradhdha*, or final rituals. The offerings for the dead are many: food, clothes, utensils, even pieces of furniture like beds. But it is also mandatory to serve the dead man's favourite dishes as part of the offerings. Once the rituals have been completed, the priest takes all the non-perishable items as his booty.

Apart from the general collection of offerings, there is a special one of cooked rice and fish, called *pinda*, without which the spirit of the dead person cannot be satisfied. Once again, it is an indication of what Bengal considers its basic staples to be. The *pinda*, usually cooked by the wife or the daughter-in-law of the deceased, is set out in separate lumps on banana leaves for all the ancestors that can be recalled. Since the denizens of the other world cannot visibly partake of mortal rice and fish, members of the subcaste of *agradani* Brahmins had to eat some of the *pinda*. Despised, considered fallen, the *agradani* appeared at the rituals for the dead like some material ghost, and one stark story tells of an *agradani*, so driven by poverty that he cannot resist gobbling up the *pinda* offered to his son. The left-overs are dumped in the nearest river after some have been scattered on the ground for the crows, who are considered the representatives of ghosts.

Once the religious rituals are taken care of, the dead person's family is obliged to invite a certain number of Brahmins and serve them with a good vegetarian lunch. Satisfying the Brahmins has been a compulsory part of many Hindu ceremonies from ancient times, as the evidence of literature shows. No Brahmin, if invited, can refuse to come. But some will eat only token mouthfuls of fruit and sweets, believing that if they eat well, they will have to share in the dead person's sins. In the evening there is another vegetarian meal to which relatives, friends and neighbours are invited. It is longer, and more formal, although the children of the dead continue with their austere meals and sleep on the floor till the thirteenth day.

Though strictly vegetarian, the *shradhdha* meals are no less tasty than those served at weddings. There is no austerity in cooking. Fried vegetables like aubergines or *patols* or even spinach form the first course. Then comes the *dal*, usually made with yellow split peas, followed by a fish-meat substitute – a rich dish made either with *chhana*, pressed cottage cheese, or with *dhonka*, squares of pressed, ground *dal*. The meal ends with the usual chutney, sweet yoghurt and *mishtis*.

Chhana is made into spicy curries all over India, but the *dhonka* is probably more typical of Bengal. The name itself is intriguing for it means hoax or deception, and the squares of *dal* are meant to deceive you into thinking you are eating meat, or at least they are meant to puzzle the eater. Of course those heathen ingredients, onion and garlic, cannot be used in a meal cooked for a funeral feast. But the spicy richness of *dhonka* leaves no sense of lack. Though it is quite time-consuming, it is worth the time and effort spent on it. The main trick is not to break the *dhonka* pieces. My first few attempts were disastrous because I insisted on stirring them; however shaking the pan gently is good enough.

Start **Dhonkar dalna** a day ahead by soaking 250 g (½ lb) of yellow split peas overnight. The following day drain the water, let the *dal* dry a little, and grind it to a very smooth paste. Coarsely ground *dal* will be a mess. Grind half a coconut, again very finely, and mix with the *dal*. The important thing is to make sure that the amount of coconut is half that of the *dal*. Season this mixture with salt, a little sugar and 1 teaspoon of ground ginger. Put it in a frying pan over a low flame and stir until it is quite dry. Transfer to a greased tray or dish and press and shape into a large, flat square 2 cm (¾ in) in thickness. Cut this into small 2.5 cm (1 in) squares or rectangles with a sharp knife. Set aside. Take 250 g (½ lb) of potatoes and peel, cube and fry them in 120 ml (4 fl oz) of oil heated in your *karai* or pan. Remove and fry the *dhonka* squares in the same oil carefully until they are brown. Remove and set aside.

Throw in 1 teaspoon of whole cumin and 2 bay leaves as *phoron*. As soon as they turn brown, add 3 teaspoons each of ground ginger, cumin and coriander, a little salt, 2 tablespoons of yoghurt and 2 teaspoons of sugar. Fry these over a high heat for two to three minutes. Add your fried potatoes, stir for another two to three minutes and pour in 250 ml (8 fl oz) of water. Bring to the boil and keep covered over a medium heat until the potatoes are cooked. Uncover, turn the heat to high and add 120 ml (4 fl oz) of coconut milk. As the gravy thickens, add the *dhonka*. As soon as this comes to the boil, add 2 teaspoons of ground *garom mashla* with 3 teaspoons of roasted chilli-cumin powder and 2 teaspoons of ghee. Gently shake the pan and let all the flavours mingle before removing from the stove. Check the salt and sugar balance and add if necessary. In East Bengali households they garnish this dish with chopped coriander leaves. Less chilli-cumin powder can be used if it seems too hot.

Sheet

WINTER

Brief, invigorating, with vibrant colour standing out in a dry and rough landscape, winter in Bengal is like the perfect love affair. It is our season of mists and mellow fruitfulness, two short months of bliss. The flowers of winter are not like the demure white blossoms of the monsoon and the autumn. Crimson roses, yellow and bronze chrysanthemums, blazing marigolds and multicoloured dahlias clamour for attention.

In the country you can feast your eyes on fields of mustard awash in yellow blossom, on patches of maroony-red *lalshak*, on the subtle greens of cabbages in the earth and the climbing vine of the *lau* spreading over thatch roofs and bamboo frames. In the city markets the rich, purple aubergines are offset by snowy-white cauliflowers peeking from within their leaves; carrots, tomatoes, beets, cucumbers, spring onions and bunches of delicate coriander leaves invite you to stop cooking and make salads. And the infinite variety of leafy greens – spinach, mustard, *laushak, betoshak, lalshak, methishak, muloshak* – makes you wonder if the impoverished Hindu Bengali widow is to be pitied or envied for her vegetarian diet.

The most important and joyful thing about winter to a Bengali is the opportunity and ability to eat far more abundantly than during any other season, to indulge in all the rich meat, prawn, egg and fish dishes that sit too heavily on the stomach at other times of the year. The colonial years have left behind the festivities of Christmas and New Year, enthusiastically adopted by Bengalis, and the early winter month of Poush sees the *pithaparban*, a folk festival designed specifically for the making and eating of large quantities of sweets. And even if a family cannot afford too much of these, there is still a wonderful array of vegetables and fruits from which to choose.

This is also the time for the outdoor-shy Bengali to venture out for a day at the zoo or at the races, or a day in the country where picnic lunches are eaten as in an impressionist painting. The grass, almost too dry, is a welcome change after the sogginess of the monsoon, and village children often get a fire going under a large tree and cook themselves a rough meal of rice, *dal* and vegetables, all cooked in the same pot, a meal called *choruibhati*, literally rice for the sparrows. The lambent sunshine is quite a contrast to the searing heat of summer and after a meal eaten in the open, it is only natural for the indolent Bengali to have a little snooze under the light-and-shade canopy provided by the branches of large trees. Most trees in Bengal are not deciduous and so retain their leaves, though these become dry and browned with dust.

For all the continuity of the Bengali eating tradition, many of the vegetables which signal winter to us did not feature in the Bengali diet three or four centuries ago. Mukundaram Chakrabarti's sixteenth-century narrative poem, *Chandimangalkabya*, contains a passage in which Shiva, on a winter morning, asks his wife Gouri to cook him an elaborate vegetarian meal. The menu of his desire consists of a bitter *shukto* made with aubergines, *shim* (a kind of buttery-textured bean) and margosa leaves as a first course; a combination dish of aubergines, our native pumpkin, *sari* (a kind of elongated taro), jackfruit seeds and *phulboris*, all seasoned with the juice of ginger; mustard greens and *betoshak* fried in pungent mustard oil; fried *phulboris* soaked in syrup; two kinds of *dal*, one slightly sweet, made with yellow split peas, the other lentils with lemon juice; a sweet chutney of sour *karamchas*; a *ghanto* made with *maan*, jackfruit seeds and *boris*, all flavoured with a *phoron* of cumin fried in ghee; and finally, spinach cooked with a sour fruit, *amra*.

Shiva's menu is extraordinarily elaborate, but it does not seem alien because the ingredients are still around and the basic methods of cooking vegetables have not changed all that much. Where, however, are the cabbages, cauliflowers, potatoes, tomatoes, beets or green peas? Nowhere in sight, and the Bengali managed very well without them. As I have said in the previous chapter, many vegetables which are now part of the daily diet, were imported into Bengal during the sixteenth and seventeenth centuries by Dutch, French and Portuguese traders. Though it is often hard to determine which vegetable was brought in by whom, potatoes, most scholars concede, were a Portuguese contribution. When the British became the rulers of India, their eating preferences also influenced the cultivation and marketing of these 'foreign' vegetables. Tomatoes, called 'English aubergine', used in fish and vegetable recipes to create a sweet-and-sour taste, can definitely be attributed to the British presence. The concept of serving raw vegetables as salad too, was introduced by our colonial rulers. Throughout the eighteenth and nineteenth centuries, the culinary genius of Bengal slowly developed the modern vegetarian classics by combining the old and the new. Cabbages, potatoes and peas became the base for a spicy winter *ghanto* which rivals the *mochar ghanto* that has been a favourite since medieval times. Cauliflowers, combined with potatoes, were made into a rich and fragrant *dalna* that was a wonderful variation of the summer specialty, the *patol* and potato *dalna*. As for green peas, the Bengali spurned the plain boiled version served on the dinner tables of his British ruler and made delectable savouries like *matarshutir kachuri* or *chirar polao* or the fillings for samosas with them, as well as from adding them to other vegetable dishes.

The most amazing import, of course, is the potato. After the Irish, Bengalis are probably the greatest potato eaters in the world, and yet this is such a relative upstart in the hierarchy of our food. With rice, it is an inevitable daily ingredient in the diets of vegetarians and non-vegetarians alike, and at no other time does the Bengali do as much with the potato as in winter, when the small new potatoes are available in addition to the old ones. In my grandfather's house the dry potato *bhaji*, tiny cubed potatoes fried with *panch phoron* and whole red chillies was a compulsory item served with chapatis at dinner. In my parents' home we would sometimes have *bati chachchari* made out of julienned potatoes. This is a simple and delicious preparation, ideal for the cook who does not have much time or attention to spare. My mother would cut and wash the potatoes, mix them thoroughly with salt, a tablespoonful of finely chopped ginger, a couple of green chillies and a tablespoonful of mustard oil. The mixture would then be put in a small, tightly-covered pot, almost like a lunch box, and left on a very low flame until the potatoes were cooked and the oil and the ginger juice had mingled to add their flavours to the vegetable. Fish, meat, eggs as well as other vegetables are combined most often with potatoes.

But of course no *bhaji* or *bharta* can bring out the full glory of winter's new potatoes. Small, round, pale-skinned, these tubers would never be wasted in such preparations. Instead, they are made into different kinds of *dam*. Served with puffy, golden *luchis*, the *alur dam* transports even the most carnivorous Bengali to celestial bliss. As with the hilsa, there are many recipes for the potato *dam*, and families have their special combinations of ingredients, all of which are delicious. Apart from the simple recipe mentioned in the previous chapter, I would like to mention another one of my favourites.

 To make **Alur dam** for four, I take 500 g (1 lb) of potatoes, boil and peel them and cut them into cubes. New potatoes are left whole. I also get together 3 grated medium onions, 10–12 cloves of pasted garlic, 1½ tablespoons of tamarind extract mixed with 250 ml (8 fl oz) of hot water, 1½ teaspoons of red chilli powder, 1 teaspoon of turmeric powder, salt and sugar to taste and *garom mashla* (3 cinnamon sticks, 4 cardamoms, 4 cloves) and 2 bay leaves for *phoron*. Then I heat 60 ml (2 fl oz) of oil mixed with 1 tablespoon of ghee, fry the *garom mashla* and bay leaves in it and add the grated onion and garlic. When these are browned, I add chilli and turmeric and, after a minute, the potatoes. These are stirred briskly until they turn brown and the spices cling to them. Then I add the tamarind water, an extra 120 ml (4 fl oz) of plain water, salt to taste and 3–4 teaspoons of sugar, bring it to a boil and simmer over a low heat until the flavours blend and the sauce thickly coats the potatoes. Finally, I check and make sure that the sweet-sour-salt balance is right. If not, I adjust it.

The new potatoes were also used by my mother, a working woman, to make a very tasty but very quick dish during the winter. She would boil and peel the potatoes. Green peas would be shelled and washed. Then she would heat some oil in her *karai*, sauté the potatoes for a few minutes, add the peas, sauté a little longer and then add several coarsely chopped large tomatoes, 3–4 green chillies and salt to taste. This would be left to simmer with a little water until the tomatoes gave up their juice and a thickish sauce coated the vegetables. Chopped coriander leaves would be added and, when the *karai* came off the fire, she would sprinkle some fresh mustard oil on the vegetables and leave them covered until it was time to serve them. Meanwhile, hot chapatis would be made.

The new potatoes of winter also figure in a *dalna* with cauliflowers, but I always preferred a lighter combination of the two, which is easy to make anywhere.

 To make this **Cauliflower bhaji**, take a medium-sized cauliflower and chop it into very small florets. The hard stem at the bottom has to be cut into tiny pieces. Cook 120 g (4 oz) of green peas and drain them. Peel 2–3 medium potatoes or 7–8 new potatoes and cut them into small cubes. You also need 1 medium onion finely chopped and 3–4 spring onions also chopped, but each kept separately. Heat some mustard oil (start with 2 tablespoons, add more later if needed) and fry the potatoes golden brown. Remove and set aside. In the same oil, throw in a *phoron* of 3–4 dry red chillies, 1 teaspoon of whole cumin seeds and 2 bay leaves. After a couple of minutes, add the onions, fry till golden brown and throw in the cauliflower. Stir once or twice, add a little salt and reduce to a medium heat. Sauté gently for three to four minutes, add the peas and fried potatoes and simmer covered over a low heat until the florets are tender. Uncover, check for salt, adding if needed, turn the heat to high and stir until the vegetables are browned. Just before removing, add the spring onions. Despite being dry, it tastes good with both rice and *luchi*.

Green peas, unknown to Shiva, are one of the most prized winter vegetables today, partly because they are limited to the

season, unlike the potatoes. Apart from being combined with
a host of other ingredients, they are made into a wonderful
savoury preparation which is a universal Bengali favourite.
This *matarshutir kachuri* also bridges regional and national
boundaries very easily. I have yet to find anyone who does not
like it. Though it is often served with a dry potato *dam*, it is
good enough to eat by itself. A *kachuri* is basically a stuffed
luchi and there are two steps to all *kachuris*, the filling and
the dough.

 To make the filling for **Matarshutir kachuri**, take shelled
uncooked green peas (*matarshuti*) and grind them to a
paste with a little water (enough to make 120 g (4 oz) of
paste). Add a little salt and 1 teaspoon of roasted
chilli-cumin powder and fry the mixture lightly in a frying
pan with 2–3 teaspoons of mustard oil. When the paste
cools, divide it into 12–14 little balls.

Mix 250 g (½ lb) flour with 2 tablespoons of peanut oil
and a pinch of salt. Slowly add enough water to make a
sticky dough which has to be kneaded for ten to twelve
minutes until it is elastic, like that for *luchi*. Divide this into
twelve to fourteen portions, pat each between the palms
and press to form thick flat discs. One portion of the filling
goes into the centre of each disc and is carefully covered by
stretching the dough over it from all sides like a pouch.
Once all the discs are filled and set out on a large tray, start
rolling them out carefully so that the *kachuri* is as thin as
possible, without the filling bursting out. This requires
much practice to do well. When four or five have been
rolled out, put a small *karai* on the stove and heat some
mustard oil (some people prefer to fry their *kachuris* in
ghee or peanut oil). Once the oil is hot, reduce the flame to
medium and start frying the *kachuris* as you would *luchis*.
Slide them gently along the side of the *karai*, so that they
do not land with a splash in the hot oil. As each one swells
up, turn it over with the spatula, press gently so that the
inside will be done, and lift it out on a holed spatula so that
no excess oil lingers on it. Keep rolling and frying the rest

of the *kachuris* until all are done. If the oil in the *karai* turns too dark, replace it with some fresh oil. Fried *kachuris*, like *luchis*, must be left uncovered on trays. If they are heaped together in a bowl, or covered, they will generate moisture and lose their lovely crispness.

Flattened rice, *chira*, is combined with winter vegetables to make another delightful savoury, which is served as often at breakfast as at teatime. This *chirar polao* is far less laborious, and can be made anywhere since packaged *chira* is sold in Indian grocery stores and our winter vegetables are the standard ones in the West.

 To make **Chirar polao** for three to four people, take 250 g (8 oz) of *chira*, throw out any impurities and wash it in a colander by pouring hot water over it several times. Leave this softened *chira* covered until it becomes dry and fluffy. Meanwhile, take 2 medium potatoes, peel and cut them into very small cubes. Take a small head of cauliflower and cut it into tiny florets, discarding the hard stem. Finally shell 120 g (4 oz) of green peas and steam them for a few minutes till they are done. Heat 120 ml (4 fl oz) of oil in a *karai*, fry the potatoes and cauliflower until brown, remove and set aside. Add 2 sticks of cinnamon, 3 cardamoms, 3 cloves as well as 2 teaspoons of *posto* and 2–3 whole green chillies into the hot oil. Add the *chira* and steamed green peas. Fry these for two to three minutes before adding the cauliflowers and potatoes with some salt. Stir the whole thing for about five to six minutes before removing and serving it hot. In some families a garnishing of *kari* leaves (normally used in south India) is to be seen in *chirar polao*.

Unlike the exotic vegetables brought in by foreign traders, spinach has been around for centuries. All the medieval and even pre-medieval literary passages that contain descriptions of food mention many different ways of cooking spinach,

and even today Bengalis prize this as the chief *shak* of the
winter. When it is time to bid farewell to the season it is the
spinach that is eaten in a symbolic meal. This is on the day
after Saraswati Puja, a festival which is the official harbinger
of spring. It is the sixth day, *Shashthi*, of the spring moon, and
it is qualified by the adjective *sheetal* or cool. In our house a
compulsory item of food was the *gotasheddho*. The simplest
of dishes, its flavour depends not on spices or the hand of a
master, but on natural ingredients. The term literally means
boiled whole, and that is exactly what it is. New potatoes in
their jackets, green peas in pods, tiny aubergines, sometimes
shim, and, above all, spinach that has grown old enough to
put out a budding stalk are all boiled in salted water with
whole green chillies. When done, spoonfuls of pungent
mustard oil are lavishly added to it.

Throughout the season, however, the fresh, young leaves
of the spinach are eaten in countless different forms, but one
of the most interesting dishes requiring spinach was
introduced to our house by Sadhubaba, an old man venerated
as a guru by my grandfather. One of his favourite items was
an unusual *khichuri* which in our family went by the name of
bhoutik khichuri, *bhoutik* meaning supernatural. Spinach
was added to the basic rice and *dal* of the *khichuri*. The green
astringency of the spinach was accentuated by a little sliced
karola, bitter gourd, some green peas and cubed potatoes, all
seasoned with ground ginger and ground black pepper. The
greenish *khichuri* was a great contrast to the golden look of
all other kinds of *khichuri*. The mild bitterness, occasionally
interrupted by the bitingly sharp green chillies, also made a
welcome change from our richer version of winter *khichuri*
where cauliflowers, green peas, potatoes and the *shim* were
cooked with the rice and *dal* and where lots of ghee, cumin
and *garom mashla* were used. Both kinds of *khichuri*
provided wonderfully nutritious meals for our vegetarian
guests. But in our family we seem to have a greater
inclination for the supernatural, and thirty years after
Sadhubaba's death, my mother and her sisters still make

bhoutik khichuri with pleasure and nostalgia.

Many of the guests who came to our house during Sadhubaba's visits were devout Vaishnavs and strict to the point of being vegetarians. Though *khichuri* and other vegetables were commonly served to them, sometimes *luchis* would be made for dinner and some special vegetable dish would be the accompaniment. In the winter one of the prized items was the *ghanto* made with cabbage, *bandhakopi*. There are many variations in *phorons* or the proportion of spices used in different families, but years of trial and error have made each variation delicious.

To make **Bandhakopir ghanto**, take a cabbage weighing 500 g (1 lb) and discard the top 3–4 leaves. Quarter it and chop each quarter very fine, almost shredding it. Discard the hard central stem portion. All *ghantos* require finely chopped vegetables. Take 3–4 small potatoes, peel and cube them. You also need 120 g (4 oz) of shelled green peas. For the seasoning, get together ground *garom mashla* (3 sticks of cinnamon, 3 cardamoms, 4 cloves), 1 teaspoon each of turmeric and chilli powder, 1½ teaspoons of ground ginger, 1 teaspoon each of ground cumin and coriander, plus salt and 3–4 teaspoons of sugar. Put the cabbage in a pot with a little water and steam it over a medium heat for three to four minutes. Heat 3 tablespoons of mustard oil in a *karai* and fry the potatoes golden brown. Remove and set aside. Then throw in a *phoron* of 1 teaspoon of whole cumin and 2 bay leaves. This can be substituted by a *phoron* of asafoetida or *panch phoron*. After a minute or so, add the ground spices, fry for a few minutes and add the cabbage, carefully pressing out the water before putting it in. Cook with spices for three to four minutes and add the potatoes, green peas, salt and sugar. Stir thoroughly and leave covered over a medium heat until the potatoes are tender. Taste for salt and add the ground *garom mashla* and 2 teaspoons of ghee. Sometimes my mother adds tomatoes which lend their colour and tartness to the dish.

This *ghanto* is also very good with rice. Sometimes, for a change, we would have cabbage very lightly fried with a *phoron* of *kalo jeera* and seasoned with salt, sugar and green chillies. Chopped coriander would be added at the end. At other times cabbage would become non-vegetarian (though never for Sadhubaba's devotees) and be cooked with meat or with a large head of carp. Needless to say, it was the men in our family who clamoured for these complicated pre-parations.

Though all these vegetable dishes are common among the Hindus and though most of them are our family favourites, I cannot talk about winter vegetables without mentioning an aubergine recipe made for me in Dhaka by my friend Nusrat. Aubergines are available through the year, but it is in winter that you find the largest and fleshiest purple ones. These are often made into *begunpora*, which I have described earlier. But it is in Bangladesh, in a village called Gaffargaon in the district of Mymensingh, that the tastiest aubergines appear during the winter. So bursting with flesh are they that the normal elongated shape is changed almost to a round one.

 To make **Beguner tak** (or aubergine with tamarind), Nusrat took a large purple aubergine and cut it vertically into thick portions, leaving them joined at the end, the same way we do for *begunpora*. About 10 cm (4 in) of the stem was also retained to facilitate handling. She rubbed the aubergine inside and outside with a touch of salt and 1 teaspoon each of turmeric and chilli powder. Then she heated oil, 360 ml (12 fl oz), in a large pot and fried the aubergine so that all sides were equally fried, and parted the slices with a spatula several times to fry the inner flesh. Once the whole thing was soft and brown, she lifted it out and kept it in a large serving bowl. Then she chopped 10 small onions very finely and pasted enough garlic to make 2 tablespoons. She blended tamarind pulp and water to have 4 thick tablespoons of it. Whole cumin and coriander seeds had been roasted before and kept in bottles and she was going to use some of it at the end. When all these spices were ready, she heated the same oil in the pot and sautéd the onions until light brown. Then she added 3 teaspoons each of turmeric and chilli powder, the garlic paste and a little salt and fried the mixture for about five minutes, stirring constantly. To this was added 120 ml (4 fl oz) of water and the mixture kept on the flame for five more minutes, being stirred from time to time. Then she added the tamarind pulp and 1.2 l (2 pints) of water. As soon as it came to a boil, the aubergine was lowered into the pot and left to cook on a medium flame for about twenty minutes. During this time she would let the juices enter evenly. When she judged the aubergine to be ready, she added 6 tablespoons of sugar and let it cook uncovered for five more minutes. At this stage the sauce tends to stick to the bottom and she kept gently scraping the pot without dismembering the aubergine. Finally, she tasted the salt and removed the pot. If you find your sauce still watery at this stage, you can keep it on the fire a little longer. And if it becomes too dry, a little water can be added. A final addition of 2 teaspoons each of the roasted cumin and coriander powder, and the dish was ready. This tart and spicy dish is served usually at lunchtime together with *polao* and various meat and hilsa dishes.

Apart from major vegetable dishes featuring in main meals, winter vegetables are also used as the filling for a savoury snack which is a favourite throughout the year, the *shingara*. These triangular creations of a thin shell enclosing seasoned, fried vegetables are to be found in every neighbourhood teashop. In the West they are better known as *samosas*, a term we reserve for *shingaras* with a meat filling. You can also find them in some sweet shops, for the perfect idea of a quick tea is hot *shingaras* and sweet, spongy *rosogollas* accompanied by several cups of hot sweet tea. In Dhaka my husband and his friends often reminisced to me about their college and university days. One of the things that provoked great nostalgia was the *shingara* sold at Madhu's Canteen, a teashop inside the university campus. For the traveller, the best places to try *shingaras* would be not the big sweet shops or the restaurants, but the roadside teashops. The only thing to watch out for is whether there are plenty of customers there, for that is a sure sign of good food. And if he chooses his time well, early in the morning when the first pot of tea is brewed, a few hours later when it is time for a mid-morning break, or at teatime in the afternoon, he will find the *shingaras* being fried right in front of him. Nothing can equal the taste of freshly-made *shingaras*. Sometimes, small town teashops will make better *shingaras* than those in large cities like Calcutta. I will always remember the extraordinary taste of the *shingaras* served in two small towns – Bolpur in West Bengal, where I found them in the student canteen on the campus of Shantiniketan, and Barisal in Bangladesh where I was taken to the legendary sweet shop called Gharbaron where both *shingaras* and *rosogollas* came in magnum sizes.

Like all savouries, the *shingara* also varies a lot depending on who makes them. The shell for an ordinary *shingara* can be made with a dough similar to that for *luchi*. Each disc is cut into half and a portion of filling is placed on each half, which is then folded over and sealed at the edges to resemble a triangle. In winter the filling consists of tiny cubed potatoes, green peas, peanuts and raisins, or potatoes, green peas and tiny bits of cauliflower, all fried together either with *panch phoron* or with a bit of chopped onion or some cumin seeds. The stuffed *shingaras* are then deep-fried like *kachuris*. Of course, the shell can be very rich and flaky too, like a good pastry shell. Sabu, the bald, irascible, paan-chewing, maniacal cook I had in Dhaka, used to make meat-filled *shingaras* for my guests when he happened to be in a good mood. But he always guarded the recipe jealously, so I could never learn how the shell was so many-layered and flaky, how the meat inside was so finely shredded yet juicy, and what combination of spices he used.

In this tropical region winter is not only the time to eat well, but also to sleep well. The beautiful days of gentle sunshine tempt anyone who has leisure. Quilts and blankets are spread out over balcony rails to collect the warmth of the sun all day. Even the midday sun is so merciful that it is no longer the proverbial mad dogs and Englishmen who will brave it but mild old people and hard-working housewives who will sit on balconies or porches and soak up the sun. At night there is the happiness of snuggling under the warmed quilts after a relished hot meal, and though there is nothing like the pleasure of sleeping late on a chill winter morning, there are compensations for foregoing that. I can still remember waking up very early and going up to the roof of my grandparents' house. Everything would be shrouded in a pale mist and noise of the city traffic seemed strangely absent, the silence punctured from time to time not by the birds but by the distant foghorns of ships in the harbour. Though different from the magical evocations of a monsoon day, the shrouded silence of such mornings has its own undeniable sense of mystery. Once on the steamer coming back from Barisal to Dhaka, I happened to wake up at four o'clock in the morning and went out on deck to find that we were completely becalmed by an impenetrable white fog. I experienced the true meaning of isolation and silence as the chilly fog enveloped me, and it was hard to believe that this was tropical Bangladesh, not some cold northern country.

In my grandparents' house winter was the time to really enjoy all the 'hot' foods which were taboo in the summer. Eggs, being 'hot', featured prominently in the diet in many different forms. For a long time Hindu Bengalis ate only duck eggs. Chicken being a heathen bird, the prohibition extended to its eggs. Duck eggs, however, had a pronounced odour which made it difficult to eat them boiled, fried or poached, so they had to be made into an omelette at breakfast or a gravy-based *dalna* when served at lunch or dinner. The Bengali omelette bore no resemblance to the soft, fluffy French ones, so tremulous in the middle, which Europeans savour with ecstasy. Ours were fried in pungent mustard oil to an almost leathery consistency and flavoured with chopped onions and fiery green chillies.

By the time I was old enough to have distinct preferences, the chicken and its egg had become part of our household diet. Hen's eggs went on acquiring greater popularity over time not only because of increased availability and growing size, but also because of a strange conviction that they were less 'hot' than duck eggs. Later, when I was living in Bangladesh, I found a curious application of the same belief. Duck eggs were absolutely forbidden to nubile young girls in many villages because of the conviction that the 'heat' would turn their innocent thoughts in dangerously lascivious directions. But as poultry farming has made both chicken and its eggs more affordable, the mythical properties of duck eggs have begun to fade in people's memories. One of the most striking instances of indigenisation of foreign foods that I have come across in Bengal is French toast. I, like so many other Bengalis, had known it to be a savoury snack, golden slices of bread, dipped in a mixture of whipped egg, salt, onion and green chillies and fried in our usual mustard oil. Imagine my surprise when I found a meek, mild and sweet preparation masquerading under that name at the American breakfast table.

The most pleasant surprise I had with eggs was in Bangladesh, during my first experience of the great Muslim festival of Shab-e-Barat, night of destiny. On this night, all devout Muslims are supposed to visit the cemeteries where their family members are buried, to light incense sticks and say special prayers. These observances are important because on this night the fate of every believer is determined in heaven for the coming year. For an outsider like myself the most memorable aspect of Shab-e-Barat was the quaint custom of eating bread (mostly made with rice flour) with different kinds of *halua* on the following day. Most households will make huge quantities of bread (flat discs like chapatis) and distribute them to beggars who come in droves. This obligatory sharing of food on festive days with those who possess nothing is one of the most beautiful aspects of Islam.

It was only on that occasion that I realised what infinite variety and skill goes into the making of *halua*. It could be made out of flour, arrowroot, ground yellow split peas, eggs, carrots, gourds and even meat. One thing which all *haluas* have in common is that they are cooked in ghee and heavily sweetened. Some of this bewildering array was on display in the houses I visited on that day, and the taste of them, eaten in succession, was like an ascending scale of notes, but to my mind the tastiest and one of the easiest *haluas* was that made with eggs.

 To make this **Dimer halua**, you take 8 eggs, 175 g (6 oz) of sugar, 120 ml (4 fl oz) of evaporated milk, 120 ml (4 fl oz) of ghee, 3 whole cardamoms and 3 pieces of cinnamon, 2.5 cm (1 in) long, and a pinch of saffron. First soak the saffron in 2 teaspoons of milk in a cup. Break the eggs into a large bowl and whip until the yolks and the whites are smoothly blended, though it should not be frothy. Then pour the rest of the ingredients slowly into the bowl. Mix smoothly. Taste a little for sweetness, adding sugar if needed. Then transfer the mixture to a thick-bottomed pan or *karai* and put it on a low flame. Stir constantly, making sure the *halua* does not stick or burn. Gradually the whole thing will be transformed into tiny yellow granules. As soon as all the moisture has evaporated and the sheen of the ghee is visible, remove from the stove. Delay will make the *halua* harden with heat. Chopped almonds and pistachios can be used for garnishing. Some people even add raisins to the mixture before cooking. If you do not like saffron, you can add a few drops of rose-water.

My sister-in-law would sometimes make a variant of this which was firmer in consistency and could be shaped into diamonds or squares. It tasted divine on a wintry morning with *parota*. It is also an ideal tit-bit to serve the occasional guest, for it keeps better than the *halua*.

For **Dimer borfi** she would take her eggs, 8 of them, and separate the whites from the yolks. Then she would whip the whites until they were absolutely stiff. The yolks would also be whipped into creamy smoothness and the two would be mixed together. To this she would slowly add 500 g (16 oz) of sugar. Next 250 ml (8 fl oz) of ghee would be heated in a pan and the egg mixture, flavoured with rose-water or saffron, would be poured in and kept over a low flame. After that it was a matter of stirring and stirring until your arm was ready to fall off. This one has to be cooked much longer than the other one, until it really starts sticking to the pan. The colour too will be different. When she found she could not cook it any longer without burning the mixture, she removed it from the stove and transferred it to a flat tray or serving dish. First it would be shaped into a rectangular piece, 0.6 cm (¼ in) thick, and then criss-cross cuts would be made to form diamond-shaped *borfis*.

Such memories of rich food in winter also take me back to the Bangladeshi village during this season. Going to Dapdapia, my husband's home village in Barisal, was a very different pleasure during the astringent crispness of the Bengali winter. None of the magical lushness of the monsoon was in evidence. No river in full spate, nor ponds brimful of water and water weeds. The *kutcha* roads were dusty beneath our feet as we walked from the landing place to the family home. This, of course, was not a traditional thatched cottage but a concrete structure built by one of my brothers-in-law for occasional visits to the village. The ancestral home stood close by, though it was in very poor condition. Next to it was an overgrown plot of land where my father-in-law lay buried, but no ghostly presence marred my pleasure in that wintry landscape where the large trees had lost some of their leaves, the earth looked dry and brown and yet burgeoned with various crops, and the *khejur* trees stood in rows with earthen pots tied to their trunks to catch the *ras* or sap as it trickled from the tapping cuts.

The morning after our arrival in Dapdapia I woke up to find the shutters raised from without and several pairs of curious eyes looking at us. When I came out, the group of giggling girls scattered in haste, but not before one of them had invited me to our cousins' house for breakfast. It was a short walk across the garden, but that was the first time my bare feet sank into soft grass wet with the tender dew of a winter morning. As often happens, it had been misty earlier, and I saw the moisture gleaming in glassy beads on the shrubs and branches. That breakfast was the first time I tasted the pure, undiluted sap of the date-palm, naturally chilled in its earthen pot from exposure to the night air. It is the most natural and uncloying sweetness that I have ever encountered.

As a child I had heard my father talk about drinking this *khejur ras* straight from the tree. In fact village boys often incur the wrath of farmers who have tied their pots to the trees by climbing up and drinking the *ras*, quietly replacing the pot and disappearing. Though the date-palm tree looks the same round the year – a shorter, less attractive cousin of the tall coconut – the best sap is generated only during the winter. The first tapping takes place in late autumn and successive tappings go on throughout the short winter. Some parts of Bengal provide better habitats for the date-palm and the coconut tree than others. The districts of Barisal, Faridpur and Khulna are particularly well known for their date-palm trees and a popular adage in Bangladesh says that the district of Fardipur is noted for its thieves, swindlers and *khejur gur*! But though the trunk provides such a delightful sweetener, the actual dates from the date-palm tree are nowhere near as tasty as those from desert climates.

The date-palm sap is made into three types of *gur*: liquid, grainy and the solid chunks of *patali*. The sap is heated in huge *karais* over wood or coal stoves and only an expert can gauge the different degrees of cooking to achieve the right textures. The arrival of *gur* in the market is the signal for the professional sweet-makers to start preparing one of their most popular products, *sandesh* flavoured with the new *gur*. This *nalen gurer sandesh* has a browny-pink tinge and is very dear to the plump Bengali's heart. At the beginning of the season, *gur* is sold in its liquid form, *jhola gur*. This comes in earthen pots and disappears fast enough. In our home it would be used rather like maple syrup in North America, poured over hot *luchis* or chapatis and as a sweetener in the milk. It ferments easily and so has to be eaten quickly. In rural areas the fermented *gur* is made into a kind of cheap liquor which tribals and poor villagers drink. It was this same *jhola gur* which inspired a committed following from exceptional Bengalis like Sukumar Ray, our version of Edward Lear or Lewis Carroll. In one of his delightful poems he spun out an absurdly contradictory list of all the good things of life, and the very best of the best was bread with *jhola gur*. The solid *patali gur* can be stored and used for quite a few months after winter is over, and refrigeration gives it even longer life. The most notable application for it is its use in *payesh*, in place of sugar. The pure nutty sweetness of the *gur* makes this winter *payesh* a Bengali gourmet's dream.

The house in the village where I had breakfast belonged to distant relatives, my in-laws, but the shyness between town and country limited our conversation mostly to smiles and nods. As I sat looking at all the activity in the large kitchen, a young girl came in with a bunch of greens and sat down in front of a *bonti* to chop them. The leaves and stems lost all character and fell in a pile of minute green fragments on the plate placed to catch them. Some of the others noticed my amazement and explained that skill at cutting this *koloi shak* was one of the factors that went in a girl's favour when the prospective bridegroom's family was appraising her. The greens were fried with chopped garlic and just before serving some dry red chillies were roasted and crumbled over them. I have never forgotten the taste nor the magic speed of the hands that went into the cutting.

Along with *koloi shak* there were many items cooked for our lunch that day, but for me the most wonderful experience was seeing the huge rui caught in the pond be made into a *jhol*. It was a beautiful specimen, weighing at least 5 kg (11 lbs), its pinkish scales gleaming in the sun as it lay gasping on the courtyard's beaten earth. The taste of a mature fish caught immediately before being cooked was ambrosial.

Evening in the village was mystery and heightened awareness. We walked out to some fields in the late afternoon to admire the vegetables and *dals* growing there against the infinite distance of a horizon unencumbered by buildings. The colours of the low-lying leafy greens were harmoniously countered by the white of the cauliflowers and the higher plants of the *dals*, the tomatoes and the aubergines. Soon the darkness came hurtling down on batwings and we hurried back to the house to pick up our shawls. Then, with one of my husband's cousins to guide us, we set out along the beaten mud tracks and raised embankments dividing the fields to eat dinner with a friend of the family at the other end of the village. The darkness was impenetrable, our only aid being the lantern carried by our guide. Above us was a most unfamiliar sky, cold, moonless and starry with no intervening veil of industrial smog. We came upon a cluster of houses and as we stepped into the courtyard-like space in the centre, doors opened on all sides and people came out with lanterns. Our guide laughed and chatted with them, and one by one the women, impelled by curiosity, came up to me and raised their lanterns to my face in a strange but unconscious parody of a priest holding a lamp to the face of his divinity.

Another plunge into the darkness of the fields, and a little later we came upon the extended homestead where Kadam Bhai lived with his family. Instead of being taken indoors, we were taken around to the back where our dinner was being cooked in the open. Two pits had been dug in the ground and a wood fire built inside each, a technique which is a tradition in many villages. Much store is set by the flavour of food cooked over a wood fire and it is generally believed to be good for one's digestion.

Huge *handis* had been placed over the flames to cook the *khichuri* and duck meat, a standard combination in Barisal and a common favourite in the winter because that is when the birds are most plump and healthy. In the old days when feudal landlords with huge properties could indulge in all kinds of gustatory refinements, the wretched birds were 'prepared' for the table to produce the extra pleasure similar to that of milk-fed veal. Several ducks, their wings clipped, would be chained to little stakes attached to a large wooden platform and kept locked up in a pitch-dark outhouse. Once a day a bowlful of rice and yoghurt would be set in front of each bird and every morning the entire platform, together with ducks, would be taken to the pond for bathing and cleaning, but the rest of the time the birds remained cooped up in the dark, unable to move or see. After two or three weeks of such treatment, the birds were considered fit for the plate, their flesh having become exquisitely soft and tender.

Though Kadam Bhai's wife was doing the cooking that evening, he himself was no mean cook. It was from him that I later learnt how to make a duck *bhuna* which always brings back to me a rush of wintry village atmosphere, the smoke from the wood fire mingling with the savoury smell of meat and spices and the sense of communal enjoyment as a group of relatives and neighbours sat down to their meal. I watched them and remembered a Bengali proverb that my mother is fond of quoting: you kill the duck for the son-in-law so that the whole family has an excuse for eating well.

Both the recipes that follow were made with wild duck. They can, however, be used for cooking chicken too, adjusting the cooking time to the type of chicken so that it has not fallen apart by the time it arrives on your plate.

 To make **Duck bhuna**, you need a nice plump bird, skinned, cleaned and cut into 12–13 portions – 2 drumsticks, 2 thighs, 2 wings, 4 breast pieces and 3–4 assorted pieces from the rest of the bird. Make sure you discard the giblets, including the stomach and liver. In a large thick-bottomed pot combine the duck with 120 g (4 oz) of pasted onion, 1 tablespoon of ground ginger, 2 teaspoons each of ground garlic, chilli, turmeric, cumin and coriander, ½ teaspoon of ground black pepper, 2 bay leaves, 3 pieces of cinnamon, 2.5 cm (1 in) long, 120 ml (4 fl oz) of mustard oil, 120 ml (4 fl oz) of water and some salt. Mix thoroughly and leave tightly covered on a low heat until the meat is absolutely tender. Stirring is not required but you should shake the covered pot gently from time to time. Remove from the fire and set aside. Chop 2 small onions and 6–7 large cloves of garlic as fine as possible. Heat 2 tablespoons of ghee in another pan, add 10–12 whole peppercorns and the chopped onion and garlic. Fry until golden brown, add the duck, stir for four to five minutes until no moisture is left and the sheen of oil is visible. Check for salt and remove. Since this is a dry preparation without much gravy, it is best to serve it with *khichuri* or *parotas*, together with a tomato, spring onion and chopped coriander salad.

Two years later, Kadam Bhai came to visit us in Dhaka. During his stay he decided to buy a couple of ducks and cook them for me, probably because he remembered my delighted appreciation in the village. This time he used a different method.

Kadam Bhai called this simply **Duck with coconut milk**. The birds were of a medium size and he set aside the fleshy portions, drumsticks, thighs, breasts. The rest – necks, wings, lower ribs, back, even heads – he put into a pan with 750 ml (1¼ pints) of water to make a stock spiced with 1 teaspoon of whole coriander seeds, a 2.5 cm (1 in) piece of ginger, a whole medium onion and a bay leaf. This he left, tightly covered, over a low flame until the meat was completely separated from the bones. Removing the pan from the stove, he strained the stock through a cheesecloth, crushing the meat to extract the last bit of juice before discarding it and the bones. Next he extracted milk from a coconut in the usual way, grinding the flesh, soaking it for half an hour in 120 ml (4 fl oz) of hot water and straining it. He was going to use double the amount of milk. Then he put a large pot on the stove and heated 175 ml (6 fl oz) of ghee in it. Into this he threw 2 bay leaves, 3 teaspoons of ground ginger, 2 teaspoons of ground coriander, 1 teaspoon each of chilli and turmeric powder and ½ teaspoon of ground black pepper. These were fried for two to three minutes and the pieces of duck were added. The meat was stirred and stirred until it became very dark brown, at which point the stock was added to cover the meat together with some salt. Duck takes a long time to cook and more stock can be added if needed. When the duck was almost done, he added the coconut milk and kept stirring over a high heat. As the gravy thickened, he added the juice of a large lemon, checked for salt and removed the duck from the stove. The rich gamy taste of the bird was successfully complemented by the sweet-and-sour touch of coconut milk and lemon. A *polao* made with fine white rice was a perfect accompaniment.

It was the wife of a colleague of my husband's who first made me a very well-known Muslim meat dish, the *handi kabab*. The name comes from the Benegali *handi*, the peculiar cooking pot, round bottomed and with a pitcher-like narrowing of the neck and a wide rim for easy handling. This dish was something I had heard about from childhood. All kababs are Muslim preparations, but somehow the *handi kabab* seemed to have an especially strong flavour of the 'other' community. Strangely, though I lived in Dhaka for almost seven years, and was invited to eat at many homes, this was the only occasion when I was given the *handi kabab*. That year, the festival of Bakr-Id had fallen in the winter and the *handi kabab* was the ideal way to prepare some of the sacrificial meat. If you don't have a *handi*, this can be made equally well in a large thick-bottomed pot with raised sides and a fitting lid.

Our hostess's method for making **Handi kabab** seemed fairly simple, but the result was surprisingly good. The meat, which was about 1 kg (2 lbs) of beef, was thinly sliced instead of being cubed and then pounded on a grinding stone. 10–12 onions were then finely chopped, lightly fried in 120 ml (4 fl oz) of oil, removed and set aside. It is important to press the excess oil out of the onions as you lift them out of the pot. In the same oil she fried 6 cloves, 2 sticks of cinnamon, 4 cardamoms, 2 bay leaves, 1 teaspoon each of whole cumin and coriander, 2 teaspoons of whole peppercorns, ½ teaspoon of crushed nutmeg and a large pinch of mace. When these were browned, she lifted them out, again pressing the oil against the side of the pot. The spices, together with the onions, were ground on the stone. A pestle and mortar or blender could be used too. Some more oil, about 60 ml (2 fl oz), was added to the pot and the pounded meat, mixed with 3 tablespoons of vinegar, was thrown into the hot oil. To this was added 2 teaspoons each of garlic and ginger paste and chilli powder, salt to taste and 250 ml (8 fl oz) of water. When all the ingredients had been thoroughly stirred once, the pot was left covered on a low flame until the meat was absolutely tender and the water had evaporated. Then she added the ground, fried spices, stirred thoroughly, kept the pot covered for five more minutes and the meat was ready to serve. This is very good with plain *polao* or with *parotas* or *luchis*.

To make **Plain polao** for eight people, take 500 g (1 lb) of Basmati rice, wash it throughly and let it drain in a colander. Get together 120 ml (4 fl oz) of ghee, 4 pieces of cinnamon, 2.5 cm (1 in) long, 4 cardamoms, 4 cloves, 2 teaspoons of pasted ginger, 1.7 l (3½ pints) of heated water, 2 tablespoons of *keora* water and salt to taste. In a large pot heat the ghee and add the cinnamon, cardamoms and cloves. Mix the ground ginger with a little water and add to the ghee. Stir a couple of times, pour in the hot water and some salt and cover the pot. As soon as the water comes to a boil, add the rice and keep stirring carefully. Let it boil for a minute or so, add the *keora* water

and cover the pot tightly. Reduce the heat to low. Keep the
pot covered for about 20–22 minutes. If the heat cannot be
lowered enough to keep the *polao* from sticking to the pot or
burning, you could put a heavy metal tray or a piece of tin
between the pot and the stove. Do not uncover or stir the
polao. After 20 minutes remove the pot from the stove and
leave covered for another 20–25 minutes before serving. To
garnish, you can finely slice some onions and fry them in
ghee until light brown. Remove them immediately from the
heat and take them out of the pan, pressing the ghee out.
Leave them scattered on a plate so that they remain dry and
crisp. To serve, dish out the *polao* on a large oval serving
dish and sprinkle the fried onions on top. This garnish is
called *bereshta* in Bangladesh. You can also put sliced
hard-boiled eggs on top and add orange or yellow food
colouring to the *polao*.

Winter, of course, is also the time when the great rivers are at
their tamest, without having totally lost their character or
potency, as sometimes happens in the hottest of summers.
River cruises on steamboats or launches are a frequent pleasure and the tranquil waters, even at the large junctions of
waterways, make the raging torrents of the monsoon an unreal
dream. Fishermen have an easy time hauling in their catch,
whether it is big fish like rui, katla or hilsa or one of the smaller
varieties, but some of the most delectable fruits of the river in
winter are several species of shrimps and prawns as well as a
kind of perch, the koi. Like the hilsa, the prawn has a specially
elevated status and this is reflected in its price. The striped tiger
prawn or *bagda chingri* is cooked with ground coconut, or
with winter vegetables or made into a *paturi* like the hilsa,
while the big, fat *galda chingri*, king prawns (like the crayfish
in the West), are cherished for their wonderful juicy taste and
added to a rich cauliflower and potato *kalia* or made into the
classic *malaikari*. Overfishing with trawlers in estuarine
waters and with nets in the rivers has made the *galda chingri*
rarer and rarer to the point of being an almost unaffordable

species. But even now, when the favourite son-in-law arrives for a visit, the Bengali parent will scour the markets for these top-heavy, moustachioed monsters to create a memorable lunch.

The *malaikari*, which makes every Bengali salivate with pleasure, is a rich red preparation in which the sauce, enriched with thick coconut milk, ghee, spices and the oozing juices from the huge heads, serves as a background to the richer red of the shells enclosing the heads. Though considered a Bengali classic, it is doubtful if the *malaikari* has been in Bengal for more than 150 years. Even Iswarchandra Gupta, the poet of good food and good cooking, who died in 1860, did not mention it. There are many theories about the origins of the name *malaikari*, which seems linked to the English word curry. By the nineteenth century it was being used for the various dishes cooked by the people of Ceylon and southern India with coconut milk, as is the modern *malaikari*, and flavoured with *kari* leaves. Another theory argues that the dish should be called Malay curry since the people of the Malay archipelago have been cooking with coconut milk for centuries, a practice which came back to us through the emigrant Indian Tamil settlers there. To my mind, however, there is a big difference between Bengali *malaikari* and similar recipes in cookbooks on South-East Asian food – this is the combination of the *garom mashla* flavour with the conconut milk and the pure ghee.

The first time my husband came to Calcutta to meet my parents was in March and my mother regretted not being able to find good enough *galda chingri*, but the next time he came it was Christmas time and she was thrilled to be able to make *malaikari* for her one and only son-in-law. He too was eager to taste her version of a preparation that he associated with his home district, Barisal. Coconut trees grow in profusion there, the soil having a high level of salinity, and cooks from Barisal revel in the use of coconut milk and shredded coconut in many dishes. I watched my mother with interest, since I had never had the nerve to try making this dish before. Though Bengali *galda chingri* may not be available elsewhere, this recipe is good for any type of shrimp or prawn.

To make the **Galda chingrir malaikari**, 1 kg (2 lbs) of
king prawns had been bought. Since their heads make up
so much of their weight, you need to buy a lot to serve
amply. In Western countries this recipe can be made with
crayfish, langoustines or even with meat taken out of a
lobster, but the pleasure we get from the juicy heads will
be absent unless the cook retains the heads and takes the
trouble of cleaning them. This is done in Bengal by
inserting a matchstick and drawing out the green bile sac
which tends to make the whole head taste bitter. The coral
is left undisturbed. Both the head and the tail with its shell
are left attached to the body which is peeled and deveined.
When cooked, the shell turns red and heightens the rich red
of the gravy. The prawns are washed, dusted with salt and
turmeric and steamed for three to four minutes (cooking
directly in water would mean draining the water together
with a good part of the coral which will ooze out).

The steamed prawns were set aside and my mother
ground the flesh of a large coconut to extract the milk from
it. A small handful of the ground coconut flesh was set
aside before 250 ml (8 fl oz) of thick milk was extracted
and diluted by the addition of 120 ml (4 fl oz) of water.
After this, 5–6 medium onions, a 5 cm (2 in) piece of
ginger and 8 cloves of garlic were ground together on the
stone. Then came the *garom mashla*, 3 sticks of cinnamon,
2.5 cm (1 in) long, 4 cardamoms and 2 cloves which were
pasted with a little water. A large *karai* was put on the
stove and 60 ml (2 fl oz) of peanut oil was heated together
with 3 tablespoons of ghee. The onion, ginger and garlic
paste was fried until golden-brown. To this was added 1
teaspoon of turmeric powder, 2 teaspoons of chilli powder
and half the ground *garom mashla*. After a minute of
frying these, she added the steamed prawns and stirred
them carefully until they were nicely coated with the spices.
The coconut milk was poured over them and brought to a
boil. Salt to taste and 3–4 teaspoons of sugar were added
and the *karai* kept covered over a low flame until the gravy
thickened and the prawns were tender. The final touch was
the addition of the pasted coconut and the rest of the
garom mashla. When everything had been thoroughly

blended, the gravy was tasted for the salt and sugar balance. Like all dishes made with coconut milk, the *malaikari* must have a sweetish taste. If more sugar is needed, you can add it at the end. The sauce should be rich, fragrant and red and the vivid red shells of the heads and tails of the *galda chingri* will give it an even richer look. Some people use the *bagda chingri*, tiger prawns, for their *malaikari* and they also prefer to make it white, in which case turmeric and chilli powder are omitted and green chillies are used to make it hot.

Tiger prawns are prized in Bengal for their relative fleshiness. The heads are not so big and do not make up most of the weight of an expensive commodity. They, too, are combined with the coconut, but in many different ways. The ultimate in gustatory delight is *dab chingri*, a preparation in which the prawns are mixed with a pungent mustard paste, salt, mustard oil and green chillies and stuffed inside a tender green coconut whose top has been removed and the excess water drained out. The coconut is then plastered with mud and slowly baked in a wood fire. Needless to say, this is a typical rural recipe which survived in the great feudal houses of Bengal with their huge cavernous kitchens and armies of servants to build the wood fire and clean up the ashes. In modern Bengali homes, where space is a major constraint and there are hardly any live-in servants, such elaborate arrangements are rare. In countries where the green coconut cannot be found, the *dab chingri* can only be talked about, but there is a simpler version which is not subject to any constraints provided the ripe coconut is available.

To make **Narkel chingri**, if you have 500 g (1 lb) of tiger prawns, then grind the flesh of half a large coconut. You will also need 2 tablespoons of ground mustard seeds. It is essential to have the black, pungent mustard seeds we use in Bengal, not the white or brown variety. Grind them on a stone or in a blender with a touch of salt and green chilli. The finer the paste, the better. You also need 1 teaspoon of turmeric powder, 5–6 slit green chillies, salt to taste and 60 ml (2 fl oz) of mustard oil. Rinse the prawns carefully in water after shelling and deveining them. You can discard the heads if you want. Squeeze the juice of 1 lemon over the prawns and leave for ten minutes. Rinse again in cold water. Heat the oil in your pot and throw in the prawns dusted with turmeric. After a minute or so add the ground coconut, the green chillies, ground mustard and salt to taste. Stir briskly and keep covered over a low flame, until the prawns are tender and all the flavours have mingled. Uncover, stir over high heat until any excess moisture has evaporated and remove from the flame. Add 2 teaspoons of fresh mustard oil and keep covered until it is time to serve. This is best with plain boiled rice.

Among the many cherished fishes of winter can be mentioned the koi, the shol and the magur. All of them are always bought live. Since they seem very hard to kill, living for a long time in buckets of water, it is assumed that a dead specimen must be really diseased. Legend tells of a shol that was perverse enough to live even after being roasted over a fire. A certain king, unwise enough to incur the wrath of Shani, Saturn, was persecuted by the malevolent deity until he lost everything and had to become a recluse in the forest. One day he managed to catch a shol and roasted it over a fire for his lunch. Just as he was about to eat it, the fish slipped out of his grasp and disappeared into the river.

There also are many apocryphal stories about the koi. Like the hilsa, the koi also becomes fat and oily in the winter, but despite its wonderful taste it is an even more dangerous fish than the hilsa. Not being a big fish (the large ones are not more than 20–25 cm (8–10 in) in length), it is served whole and the curved bones of the stomach can be lethal if stuck in the throat. One of my favourite koi dishes is made by my mother with the fish being first lightly fried, coated with chilli and turmeric powder and salt. It is then cooked in the juice of some grated onion and ginger. Green chillies add sharpness and flavour, and the delicate but oily sauce coats the fish lovingly as you eat it with plain rice. Iswarchandra Gupta, when commenting on the Englishman's way of eating fish, sneered at the total absence of spices when the fish is brought to the table and at the compensatory embrace of the fish by table mustard poured over it. In really good Bengali fish preparations except for *jhol*, the sauce embraces the fish with loving tenacity. The koi also features in some of the medieval *mangalkabyas*, cooked with the juice of ginger or with ground black pepper.

As the first month of winter, Poush, rolls on, the occasional north wind becomes a little too nippy in the morning and the dust flies around to settle in a pall over available surfaces. The heavy, still evening air traps smoke from the factories and open-air charcoal stoves that are still used in some houses and creates a spectral fog, but neither dust nor fog can curb the spirit of fun, for winter is the season for fairs and exhibitions. Shantiniketan in Birbhum district holds an annual Poush Mela which draws crowds from many places. In terms of food, Poush is the specific month for eating two things – one being *mulo*, a species of long white or pinkish white radish, the other being all kinds of rice-wheat-coconut based sweets described by the collective term *pitha*.

Of the thirteen festivals in twelve months that have become a Bengali proverb, the last day of Poush is probably the only one that is purely based on the pleasures of eating. In the old days when rural and feudal life meant extended families and communal festivities, there was great scope for gifted women to show off their various *pithas*. Modern urban life is sadly divorced from that, but the art of the *pitha* lives on. One of the simplest, *rasbara*, is made from pasted *kalai dal* which is whipped till very frothy, then fried in round balls and finally soaked in syrup. Another very simple *pitha*, the *chitoi pitha*, is made from rice flour mixed with water and left in a covered, heated, greased earthen saucer around which some

water is sprinkled to keep the *pitha* from being too dry.
Perhaps the most memorable *pitha* that I have ever tasted, at
the home of Professor Abdul Razzaque in Dhaka, was a
variation of the *chitoi*. A small triangular hilsa *peti* had been
baked right into it so that it had absorbed the oil and the
characteristic hilsa flavour. I doubt if many other savoury
snacks can match the delicacy of that taste. During my winter
visit to the village I had seen another kind of *pitha* being
served with the duck *bhuna*. Made with home-ground rice
flour, this was called *rutipitha* or *chaler ruti* (literally rice
bread). *Atap* rice, soaked for an hour and then dried, is
ground on the stone to make the flour. It is then sieved to get
rid of the coarser particles and salted boiling water is added
to the flour to make a sticky dough. It is then left for ten to
fifteen minutes on a pan set over a very low flame. This
indirect heat cooks the dough. The cooled dough is then
kneaded, divided into little balls which are rolled out to form
chapatis and toasted on a dry *tawa* or frying pan. Finally each
bread or *ruti* is held on a wire frame over a direct flame so
that it puffs up like a balloon and the inside is properly
cooked. Served piping hot, it is a most delicious medium to
mop up your portion of meat and sauce.

The bulk of *pithas*, however, are sweet rather than
savoury. In my childhood I looked forward to the *pulipitha*
or *pulipithe*, as we Ghotis used to say. Both my grandmother
and my mother regularly made this on the last day of Poush.
It is both heavy on the stomach and laborious to make
without the extra hands of an extended family, and yet
winter could never be complete without it. The vital
ingredient is *khejur gur* which permeates the milk and makes
this a treat you long for during the rest of the year. Since
khejur gur does not seem to be available outside Bengal (even
Indian grocery stores do not sell it abroad), the only way to
make this in the West will be to substitute white sugar for the
portion of *khejur gur* in the recipe that follows. In the
absence of *gur* a vital flavour of Bengal will be missed, but the
pitha itself will provide an essential Bengali delight.

To make **Pulipitha** (or *dudhpuli*) for a small family or for three to four guests, take 250 g (8 oz) of cream of wheat, half a coconut ground fine, 120 g (4 oz) of sugar, 900 ml (1½ pints) of whole milk, 120 g (4 oz) of solid *khejur gur* crushed coarsely and 2–3 cardamoms ground very fine. The filling is made first, by cooking the ground coconut with sugar over a low flame until it is sticky and gives off a sheen. This is cooled on a plate. The shell or *puli* is made by setting the cream of wheat to boil in 250 ml (8 fl oz) of water. When all the water has been absorbed and the cream of wheat forms a big lump, mash it with a spoon or spatula. You should be able to move it easily in the pan in a little while. Remove from the fire, let cool and divide this dough into little round balls. Take each one, flatten it in your palm, put a little coconut filling in the centre and close the shell to form small rolls tapering at the ends. This is the classic shape of the *pulipitha*. When all the *pulis* are ready, set the milk to boil in a pan. When it comes to a boil, reduce the heat and evaporate until it is reduced to about 750 ml (1¼ pints). Add the *pulis* and leave to cook over a low heat. Meanwhile, take the *gur* (or more sugar) and add to the milk. Stir once or twice, being careful not to break the *pulis* and let it cook until the *gur* and milk are thoroughly blended. Remove and pour into a serving dish. Sprinkle the ground cardamom over it.

For pious Hindus the end of Poush means the great concourse of pilgrims for the Ganga Sagar Mela on Sagar, an island in the Bay of Bengal where the Hooghly river joins the sea. On the early morning of the *sankranti* hundreds of pilgrims plunge for their ritual bath into the icy waters to ensure salvation in the next world, to wash away the sins of this world. In severe winters many elderly pilgrims die here from exposure to the cold. The holy confluence of the river and the sea has also seen some terrible things in the past. Bengali women who often miscarried or could not get pregnant easily, would often promise their first child to the sea, provided they had two safe births in succession. And hundreds of unfortunate women would be forced (through fear and social pressure) to carry out this grim promise. Sometimes a mother would come all the way with the doomed child but find herself unable to part from it. Anxious family members would then forcibly take the child away from her and throw it into the water.

This is the time when winter (what we have of it) occasionally bares its teeth. The pleasures of sleep, so intense when you have warm quilts and blankets, are denied to those who are too poor to afford them. A humorous Bengali verse describes the three stages of an inadequately covered man through a cold night. He starts out straight as the *dhenki* board which is used for threshing rice; halfway through the night he has assumed the half-moon shape of a tautly strung bow; and in the early hours of the morning he has curled up in a knot like a dog. In the villages they sometimes light fires outside cottages and warm themselves before going to bed, a luxury not possible in enclosed town houses. During such short cold spells I have often longed for the small, crackling fires of the countryside.

Though the season is such a cornucopia of new and different vegetables, there are not too many fruits available in the winter. The great exception is the orange which grows in the hilly regions of Darjeeling in West Bengal and Sylhet in Bangladesh. The Bengali orange is not the same as the Western fruit of that name. What we call an orange is the tangerine of the West. The transposition of the English name is interesting, for the word orange is derived from the Hindi and Urdu *narangi*. These round, pulpy, juicy, fragrant fruits are much prized and the fruit sellers in the markets set their prices high, knowing they will still manage to sell their quota.

In my family, the orange was mostly eaten as a fruit, the only culinary effort I have seen being the *kheer* with orange pulp made by my mother, but in Bangladesh I have eaten two wonderful orange dishes that linger vividly on my palate even after so many years. One was, to me, the unthinkable combination of the fruit with the koi fish. Unlike the French duck with orange or Polynesian meat dishes cooked with pineapple, Bengali cuisine rarely combines fruit with fish or meat. The only exceptions I have seen have been in Bangladesh, where once I had a hilsa dish cooked with pineapple and this koi with orange. The latter was made by my friend Nusrat when she invited me for lunch one beautiful winter afternoon. Having heard some of my comments about the comparative richness and heaviness of Muslim cooking versus the lightness and delicacy of Hindu cooking, she was determined to prove that Muslims could serve a meal that was both delicious and light. Amazingly, there was no meat, nor *polao*. Instead she served plain boiled rice with *moong dal* flavoured with ginger, cumin and green chilli, fried aubergines, koi with orange, aubergine in tamarind sauce and finally a mouth-watering dessert of orange-flavoured sweet rice. The tangerine pulp provided a lovely rich tint from which the dark koi and the green chillies stood out, and the sweet-and-sour taste of the pulp, with the added pungency of mustard oil, heightened the natural flavour of the koi. It was one of the best meals I have had in Bangladesh.

For this dish of **Kamala koi** (or koi with orange), there were 6 large, plump koi. The fish is eaten whole. It is scaled thoroughly and cleaned and gutted, with the back part of the head being left attached to the body. The gills are discarded. Like other fish, these koi were also dusted with salt and turmeric, fried lightly in oil and set aside. The painful part of making this dish was dealing with 6 large tangerines. Each was peeled, the sections separated and the pips and translucent cover removed so that only the inner pulp and juice remained. Then 4 medium onions were chopped finely. The other flavourings used were 3 teaspoons of pasted garlic, 1½ teaspoons of ground ginger, 2½ teaspoons of red chilli powder, salt and 7–8 green chillies slit in the middle. About 120 ml (4 fl oz) of mustard oil was heated in the *karai* and the onions were browned. All the ground spices were thrown in and stirred until they were dark brown and nearly sticking to the pot. A little water was sprinkled over them and the orange pulp added. This was stirred for three to four minutes, the spatula smashing the bigger portions, and the whole mixture was blended smoothly. Next, 250 ml (8 fl oz) of water was poured in and 2 teaspoons of salt added. When the water came to a boil, the fish were placed in the *karai* with the green chillies and left to cook until the gravy had thickened. Then each fish was turned over and the *karai* left on a high heat for two to three minutes before being removed from the stove. The salt can be checked at this point, more added if needed and a few drops of mustard oil should also be added. The fish should then be left covered till serving time. If no other fish or meat is being made then this will suffice only for three people.

The *kamala* or orange theme suggested by the fish preparation was further developed by a lovely salad made with the inner pulp of the orange sections and thinly sliced green bell peppers, a recently cultivated vegetable in this region. The final culinary delight was the *kamalar jarda* or orange-flavoured sweet rice served as our dessert. Though West Bengal has plenty of uses for rice, this kind of dessert is not at all common here. Perhaps some Muslim families with a strong tradition of elaborate cooking do make this sometimes, but I have never encountered it on the western side of the border. From a distance it looks almost like a dish of *polao* with orange food colouring added to it, but as you get closer, you see the syrup and the fruit juice enveloping the rice as well as the minute shreds of orange pulp. As for the fragrance, the combination of the rich smell of ghee and the fruitiness of the orange is amazing. The garnish of white almonds, green pistachios and brown raisins on top create the impression of a colourful patterned quilt. In Bangladesh I have also seen cooks use the additional decoration of edible silver or gold foil. Wafer-thin sheets of foil are easily shredded by hand and sprinkled over desserts.

To make the **Orange-flavoured sweet rice**, about 20 oranges were peeled, the sections separated and the pulp and juice scraped out into a waiting bowl. Enough of the peel was chopped into tiny slivers to make 120 g (4 oz). This was set aside separately. Then she measured out about 500 g (1 lb) of fine *polao* rice (Basmati will do) and rinsed it in a colander under running water. Leaving the rice in the colander, she put to boil 2.2 litres (4 pints) of water in a very large pot, adding a touch of orange food colouring to it. She added the rice to the boiling water and stirred from time to time until the rice was done. The orange peel was thrown in just before the rice was ready and kept there for a couple of minutes. The water was then drained and the rice left in the colander until it was dry. Then it was transferred to a large tray and spread out to let all lingering excess moisture evaporate. Meanwhile, she took another pot and made a syrup with 1 kg (2 lbs) of sugar and 120 ml (4 fl oz) of water. To this was added 3 sticks of cinnamon, 4 cardamoms and 4 cloves. She stirred the syrup over a low flame, until all the sugar melted. Then she added all the orange pulp and juice, and 120 ml (4 fl oz) of ghee and cooked the mixture for three to four minutes before adding the rice. This was stirred and stirred until no moisture was left and the rice gleamed with ghee, but she was careful not to let the rice burn or stick to the pot. At this stage the pot was covered tightly and left on the lowest of low flames for five more minutes. If this is difficult, you can try putting the pot in an oven set at the lowest temperature. When the *jarda* was finally done, she transferred it to a shallow silver serving dish and left it uncovered until it had cooled. Then she turned it over several times with a fork so that it would not be sticky or lumpy. It is essential for a *jarda* to be light and fluffy. Before serving she garnished it with almonds, pistachios and raisins.

Towards the end of Magh the cold can be made severe by occasional showers which are usually welcomed as a blessing for the winter crops, especially in the days before extensive irrigation. As Khana the wise woman declared, blessed is the land of the fortunate king where it rains at the end of Magh. Afternoons then become a time of pure bliss, with the worst of the dust washed away and the kindest of suns beaming from blue skies. The Bengali's post-lunch siesta becomes a thing of the past as even the most indolent person enjoys the daylight. I found it particularly pleasant to take a rickshaw and be driven around the quieter streets of Dhaka. On the balconies and porches of houses I would observe the women sitting with their long hair spread over their backs, wet and gleaming from the bath and drying in the sun. Elderly folk, well-wrapped up in shawls would be facing away from the sun, almost bending forward so that the whole stretch of their backs could be warmed by the sun. Silk and woollen clothes would be hanging from clothes lines, being warmed for the umpteenth time to get rid of all lingering mustiness.

This is also the time for developing all kinds of sniffles, colds and coughs, and in childhood we often dispensed with conventional medical treatment. For colds my grandmother would dose us with the age-old remedy of *tulsi*, a pungent variety of basil that grows abundantly in Bengal, crushed with honey in a little marble mortar reserved for such medicinal purposes. If a dry cough persisted, it was time to brew hot drinks sweetened with crystallised palm sugar or to boil dried sticks of a herb called *jashtimadhu* in water which absorbed the liquorice-like taste and flavour of the herb. In our Vaishnav house the *tulsi* had a special place since it is a plant favoured by Krishna. Rows of pots stood on the verandas and roof, with the plant growing in them, and every day each person had to eat a few leaves.

By the time winter draws to a close, good eating, increased outdoor activity and brisk weather have put the Bengali in a most contented frame of mind. As Magh comes to an end and the occasional southern zephyr sweeps over the land as a prelude to our elusive spring, Bengal clings tenaciously to the last remnants of blissful winter. The shawls, quilts and blankets are used even when not necessary and the last of the koi or the last orange enjoyed with protracted relish.

This contentment and pleasurable, even sensuous, abandonment is the perfect foil for the gentle discipline symbolised by Saraswati, Durga's daughter, the chaste white goddess of learning who comes gliding along on her regal white swan on the fifth day of the Magh new moon. She is a dual Muse, for in one hand she carries a book and in the other a *veena*, a stringed instrument similar to the sitar. Everything about her is white, including her sari, and her tranquil preoccupations make her the antithesis of her sister Lakshmi, red-robed goddess of fortune. It is commonly believed that those favoured by one goddess will be shunned by the other, and there are many amusing stories about how each one tried to establish her superiority over the other.

Perhaps it is an indication of whose favour our family sought that in my grandparents' house Saraswati was worshipped on this day with full ceremony. This was the only big *puja* I have ever seen at home. A huge image of the goddess would be bought and installed in the *dalan* or central courtyard and a priest would be hired to do the *puja* rites. From early morning the house was a bustle of activity as we all got up and took turns to bathe and put on fresh clothes. My grandmother, mother and aunts would sit at several *bontis* and slice a huge mound of fruitssuch as apples, *shakalus*, *safedas*, which together with bits of sugar-cane, bananas, dates and *kul* (a kind of plum) would be offered to the goddess. The bananas offered to Saraswati are a special type, very sweet, but full of large black seeds. The *kul* cannot be touched before being offered to the goddess. Since it has a very short season, Bengalis eagerly look forward to the goddess's arrival to receive the sanction to eat this sweet-and-sour fruit. This variety of *kul* is called a *narkel kul*. A sour red species, the *topa kul*, is made into lovely sweet pickles with *gur* or salted and dried in the sun.

Once all the fruits were ready, the incense lit and flowers brought in to be offered to the goddess, the priest would lead us through the special prayers. Strangely, the white-clad goddess comes at a time when there are no white flowers. It is the marigold, golden or pale yellow or even rusty red, that is considered her special bloom. For children, undiluted joy comes from offering up all schoolbooks to the goddess, since it is forbidden to study on this day. Instead, we would fold our palms and intone the Sanskrit *mantra* addressing the petal-white, deep-breasted goddess bedecked with snowy pearls and beseech her to grant us comprehensive knowledge. Once the flowers had been placed at her feet, we were free to break our fast before trouping out to see the neighbourhood images.

It is customary for women to wear pale yellow saris on the day of Saraswati Puja. The colour is called *basanti* in Bengali from Basanta, spring, and this is the surest indication that winter will disappear soon. New green leaves and flowers in flaming colours will usher in a changeable, brief season of fluctuating temperatures and festive weddings. But the presence of the goddess provides a natural hiatus between quiet contentment and febrile excitement. In the evening my family would get together to sing, for music is the other way to honour the goddess. Though metaphysical realisations were far from our minds, we children too were conscious of an elevated calm after the day's activities. My youngest aunt, who had a magnificent voice, would sing a Sanskrit hymn beseeching the goddess to bestow the gift of music, the highest form of art, and the slow cadence always struck a responsive chord in our grubby little hearts.

Like all other goddesses, Saraswati also leaves in the evening for the final ceremony of immersion in the river. Departing, the snow-white deity takes some human colour back with her. *Sindur* glows brightly on her forehead and her beautiful pink lips are stained crimson with the juice of spiced *paan* crushed against them. As she is moved from home or community *pandal* to truck to the river, the lavish garlands of marigold round her neck almost obscure her white sari, signalling the blazing sunshine of summer to come. Bengal sighs at the parting, for like some Royal Bengal tiger crouching potent, terrible yet splendid in the grass, summer too is waiting to pounce, behind the immediacy of spring.

GLOSSARY

AKHNI   A kind of perfumed water made by boiling several spices in a bundle until the original volume of water is reduced to a third. This perfumed water is used to cook the rice for a *polao*.

ALU   Potato.

ALUR CHOP   A kind of fried potato cake made by dipping balls of spiced mashed potatoes in batter and deep-frying in oil.

ATA   A kind of fruit with a green and black knobbly surface and creamy white flesh inside with large black seeds. Available only during the autumn.

ATAP   Literally, untouched by heat. The term denotes husked rice which has not been parboiled.

BALAM   A variety of long-grained rice from the Bangladesh district of Barisal, much prized for its taste.

BANGAL   A person from East Bengal, now Bangladesh.

BARA/BORA   Round balls of fish or vegetables, usually deep-fried.

BARSHA   The rainy season, the monsoon.

BASANTA   Spring. Also smallpox.

BHABRA   A savoury snack made with spiced, ground fermented chick-pea flour fried in oil. These used to be fairly common in parts of rural West Bengal.

BHAKTI   Literally, devotion. The medieval Bhakti movement in Bengal was started by Sri Chaitanya (also known as Nimai) who declared that god could be reached only through the deepest and purest of loves, not through knowledge or ritual.

BHASHAN   Literally, setting afloat in water. All images of gods and goddesses are put into the nearest river after the end of their particular festival.

BHOG   An offering of food given to the gods.

BIRYANI   Rice cooked with meat.

BONTI   A curved, raised blade attached to a long, flat piece of wood or a metal frame, and used for cutting vegetables, fish and meat. Knives are a relatively recent import in the Bengali kitchen. The *bonti* used for fish and meat is kept separate from the vegetable *bonti* and is called an *ansh-bonti*. The literal meaning of *ansh* is fish scales.

BORI   Small pellets of ground, spiced *dal*, dried in the sun and stored throughout the year, to be added to stews and vegetable preparations. More commonly used by Bengali Hindus.

CHAITANYA   Also called Sri Chaitanya or Nimai, the founder of the Bhakti movement in medieval Bengal. His followers were from the Vaishnav sect.

CHARAK   A summer festival in honour of the god Shiva.

CHHANA   The solid part of milk curdled by the addition of acid. *Chhana* is used to make a host of Bengali sweets.

CHHOLAR DAL   Yellow split peas.

CHINGRI   A generic term denoting all kinds of shrimps and prawns. Striped tiger prawns are called *bagda chingri*, while the top-heavy king prawns are called *galda chingri*. Very small shrimps are called *kuncho chingri*.

CHIRA   Flattened rice.

CHITOL   A large fish, with a very soft oily stomach or frontal portion, prized especially by the people of East Bengal, and a very bony back portion.

CHORUIBHATI   Literally, rice for the sparrows. The term means a picnic meal cooked outdoors, usually by children in villages.

DAB   The green coconut.

DAGA   The back portion of a fish, longitudinally separated from the front portion, *peti*. This portion is usually more bony.

DAL   A generic term denoting any kind of legumes. Bengalis eat at least six varieties of *dal*.

DALAN   A central space in a house, or a house built around such a space.

DANTA   Any kind of succulent stalk which is eaten with or without its leaves as a vegetable.

DHAN   Unhusked rice paddy.

DHENKI   Instrument for manual rice threshing, now almost obsolete. In Bengali adage, a symbol of unrewarding hard work.

DHENKISHAK   A fern-like leafy green, much prized as a vegetable among the people of East Bengal.

DHONKA   Literally, a hoax. In culinary terms *dhonkas* are made out of ground, pressed *dal* to form squares which are then cooked in a rich sauce and served in place of meat.

DOI   Yoghurt.

DURGAPUJA   The most important Hindu festival in Bengal, the three-day worship of Durga, wife of Shiva, goddess of deliverance.

GAROM MASHLA   Literally, hot spice. Usually it means the combination of cinnamon, cardamom and cloves, with black peppercorns being optional. The spices are often used whole to flavour meat dishes, and ground or pasted to add the final touch to some vegetable and meat preparations.

GHEE   Clarified butter.

GHOTI   A person from West Bengal.

GOBINDABHOG   A particular kind of fragrant, small-grained *atap* rice.

GOLAPSHORU   A similar kind of *atap* rice.

GONDHI   Literally, with smell. Used to describe a large variety of very fragrant lemon.

GOTASHEDHDHO   Literally, boiled whole. Specifically, this term means several winter vegetables boiled whole and seasoned with salt, oil and green chillies which are eaten by the Bengali Hindus on the day after the winter festival of Saraswati Puja.

GRISHMA   Summer.

GUR   Indigenous sugar. *Aakher gur* means unrefined cane sugar. *Khejur gur* means the brown sugar obtained by processing the sap from the trunks of *khejur* or date-palm tree during the winter.

HABISHANNO   Rice and vegetables boiled together in an earthen pot, prescribed for mourners after the death of a family member.

HALUA   A sweet dish made by cooking cream of wheat, eggs, flour and other things in ghee and sugar. Like the Middle Eastern halva.

HANDI   A cooking pot with a rounded bottom, slightly narrowed at the neck with a wide rim to facilitate holding. Rice is traditionally cooked in a *handi*.

HARAM   Among Muslims, a term denoting something absolutely forbidden.

HEMANTA   Late autumn, usually when the main rice crop is harvested.

ID-UL-FITR   The biggest Muslim festival, it comes after the month-long fasting of Ramadan or Ramzan.

ID-UZ-ZOHA   The second biggest Muslim festival, also called Bakr-Id in Bangladesh. This commemorates the prophet Abraham's willingness to sacrifice his son to Allah. The son was changed into a lamb, *bakri* which was sacrificed. Animals are still sacrificed on this occasion and their meat is called *korbani*, sacrificial meat.

IFTAAR   The breaking of the daily fast during the month of Ramadan among the Muslims. This is usually a light evening meal of cool drinks and snacks, preceding dinner.

ILISH   The Bengali name for hilsa.

ILSHE GURI   A very fine misty rain during the monsoon, the season for hilsa.

JALKHABAR   Usually a light afternoon snack, the equivalent of the English tea.

JAMAISHASHTHI   The sixth day after the new moon during the second calendar month, Jaishtha. Among Hindu Bengalis this is a day when the *jamai*, son-in-law, is ceremoniously invited by his parents-in-law and fed an elaborate meal and given gifts.

JANMASHTAMI   The birthday of the lord Krishna, during the monsoon.

JARDA   Perfumed tobacco, taken with betel leaves. In Bangladesh, the term also means a kind of dessert made with rice, cooked in ghee and syrup, often with shredded fruit like pineapples or oranges.

JHOLAGUR   Liquid *gur*, made by boiling the sap from the date-palm tree to a thick liquid consistency, like that of maple syrup.

KACHCHI BIRYANI   A Muslim preparation in which un-cooked rice and meat are cooked together over a very low flame.

KACHU   Any of several kinds of taro.

KACHU SHAK   The stems, not leaves, of taro, eaten as a vegetable.

KACHURI   A stuffed fried bread.

KAGAJI   A variety of lemon with a delicate fragrance, preferred in making lemonade.

KALBAISAKHI   A short, violent north-western storm, usually happening in the early part of summer.

KALI PUJA   The worship of the goddess Kali during the autumn new moon.

KALOJAM   A small berry, black on the outside and purple on the inside, available during the monsoon. The word is also applied to a sweet, a kind of *pantua* fried very dark on the outside to resemble this berry.

KALOJEERA   Literally, black cumin. A small black seed with a delicate flavour, used in the cooking of fish and vegetables. Sometimes called onion seeds in English.

KAMALA   The orange.

KAMINI ATAP   A small-grained variety of *atap* rice.

KANCHA   Raw or uncooked. *Kancha moong dal* means unroasted *moong dal*.

KARAI   A cooking pot, shaped like a Chinese wok, but much deeper, used for deep frying, stir-frying as well as for prepara-tions with sauces and gravy. The Bengali *karai* can be made of iron or aluminium, and usually has two loop-shaped handles.

KARAMCHA   A pinkish-white, very sour berry available during the monsoon. Used in making sour fish dishes or chutneys and pickles.

KAROLA   The larger variety of bitter gourd.

KASUNDI   A sour mustard pickle, usually made in the summer, eaten with rice and fried vegetables.

KATLA   One of the several kinds of freshwater carp.

KEORA WATER   Artificially perfumed water used in Muslim meat and rice dishes.

KHASHI   The castrated goat.

KHEER   Evaporated milk.

KHICHURI   Rice and *dal* cooked together with a variety of spices. Usually associated with the rainy season.

KHOI   Popped rice.

KOI   A kind of fish, served whole, sometimes called a climbing perch. Mostly available in the winter.

KOJAGORI   The night of the autumn full moon, when the goddess Lakshmi is worshipped. The term literally means 'who is awake' and devotees are not supposed to sleep that night.

KORBANI   Sacrifice, sacrificial meat.

KRISHNA   An incarnation of Vishnu, the second of the Hindu trinity. The Vaishnav sect in Bengal are devotees of Krishna. The word literally means black or dark, and Krishna is supposed to have been dark.

KUL   A plum-like fruit available in the winter. The sweet variety is called *narkel kul* and is used as an offering to the goddess Saraswati, while the sour *topa kul* is used to make pickles and chutneys.

KUMOR   The potter.

KUMRO   The pumpkin. *Chal kumro*, literally pumpkin on the roof, is a native Bengali gourd. The pumpkin was a late import and was originally called *biliti* or foreign *kumro*.

LAKSHMI PUJA   The worship of the goddess Lakshmi, goddess of wealth and prosperity, on the autumn full moon.

LANGCHA   A kind of sweet, like a *pantua*, but shaped like a bolster.

LANGRA   A variety of mango, much prized all over India.

LAU   The favourite Bengali gourd, pale green on the outside and white inside. Believed to have cooling properties and to be a preventive against cholera.

LUCHI   A circular fried bread, either puffy like a balloon or flaky.

MAAN KACHU   A kind of very large white taro, prized for its delicacy of taste and its supposed beneficial qualities. The word *maan* also means repute.

MACHH   Fish.

MACHHER JHOL   Fish stew.

MAGUR   A kind of fish of the catfish variety.

MALAIKARI   A preparation of prawns made with coconut milk.

MALOMASH   Literally, inauspicious month. Hindu weddings are forbidden during certain specified inauspicious calendar months.

MALPO   A home-made sweet.

MALSHA   An earthen pot in which rice, *dal* or vegetables are cooked, especially for ritual purposes.

MASOOR DAL   The lentil.

MATAR DAL   *Dal* made from green peas.

MATARSHUTI   Green peas. *Matarshutir kachuri* has ground green peas as the filling inside the bread.

MELA   A fair.

MIRGEL   A smaller variety of carp.

MISHTI   Sweet (adjective) or sweets (as a collective noun).

MISHTI DOI   Sweet yoghurt.

MOA   Round balls of puffed rice or popped rice, sweetened with date-palm sugar or white sugar and sometimes flavoured with *kneer* and cardamom seeds.

MOCHA   Banana blossom.

MOIRA   The professional sweet-maker.

MOONG DAL   A kind of small-grained yellow pulse, also called mung beans in English. They are cooked plain or after being roasted in a metal pan.

MUITHYA   A term used by the people of East Bengal to

denote fish balls made by shaping them in the fist or *muthi*.

MULO   The native radish, available during the winter.

MURI   Puffed rice.

MUROR DAL   A preparation combining roasted *moong dal* with a *muro* or fish head and spices.

NABANNO   Literally, new rice. A rural festival, especially among the Hindus, to celebrate the harvesting of the main rice crop during the autumn.

NALENGUR   The new *gur*.

NARKEL   The ripe coconut. *Narkel chingri* is a dish of prawns cooked with ground coconut.

NECHI   Small balls of dough which are patted between the palms before being rolled out.

NEEM, NEEMBEGUN   The margosa tree, whose small, bitter leaves are considered beneficial to the health during the spring and the summer. The leaves are fried crisp and combined with tiny pieces of aubergine to make *neembegun*, a first item served with rice.

PAAN   Betel leaves. These are spiced with betel nuts, cardamoms, fennel seeds, lime solution and sometimes tobacco, and chewed after a meal as a chaser. Real addicts will have *paan* with tobacco many times a day, like smokers.

PANCH PHORON   Literally, five flavours. Usually a combination of five whole spices, cumin, *kalojeera*, mustard, fennel and fenugreek. Mostly used to flavour *dal*, vegetables and fish preparations. A great favourite with Hindu Bengalis.

PANDAL   An area covered with an awning over bamboo frames in which the image of a god or goddess is placed for community worship. *Pandals* are also made for weddings and other festivals, mostly to feed people.

PANTABHAT   Left-over fermented rice, eaten by the poor out of necessity, but also considered cooling and beneficial in the summer.

PAPOR   The Bengali word for *papadam*, thin sheets of spiced ground *dal*, dried in the sun or in an oven, and fried just before serving.

PAROTA   The Bengali word for *paratha*. Fried bread,

circular or triangular in shape, often with two or three layers, but sometimes more. The famous *Dhakai parota* is as flaky as the best pastry and can have fifty layers.

PATALI GUR   The solidified sap of the date-palm tree, made by repeated boilings. This usually keeps for a few months after it has been made.

PATISHAPTA   A home-made sweet, like crêpes, usually stuffed with ground coconut and *khejur gur*.

PATOL   A small, green gourd-shaped vegetable mostly available during the summer and monsoon and considered a great favourite.

PATURI   Anything cooked wrapped in a leaf (*pata*) and left over a slow flame or stuck in the embers of a coal stove.

PAYESH   Anything, usually rice, cooked in milk.

PETI   The front or stomach portion of a big fish.

PHALAHAR   Literally, a meal of fruit. Usually this means fruit combined with popped rice or flattened rice and yoghurt or milk. Often served during the summer because it is believed to keep the system cool.

PHAN   The gruel drained out after cooking rice.

PHORON   A flavouring agent. All *dals* are first boiled in water, then flavoured with a specific combination of spices fried in oil or ghee.

PHULBORI   A particularly light *bori*, made with ground *kalai dal*.

PINDA   Literally, a lump. Usually this means an offering of cooked rice and fish, made into little balls and set out to appease the ancestors and the dead person during the Hindu funeral. A dead person's soul cannot be set free from earthly longings without this offering.

PITHA   Sweet or savoury items made from rice or cream of wheat, usually during the winter when the newly harvested *atap* rice is ground to make the flour.

PITHAPARBAN   The winter festival of making *pithas*.

POLAO   The Bengali word for pilaf.

POSTO   Poppy seeds.

PUISHAK   A succulent leafy green with a slightly astringent taste, available during the monsoon. Considered non-vegetarian, and therefore forbidden to Hindu widows who have to be strict vegetarians.

PUJA   Among Hindus, the act of worship. Religious festivals for particular gods are also called *pujas*. In Bengal, however, the word by itself also denotes the biggest festival of the year, Durgapuja.

PULIPITHA   A kind of stuffed *pitha* in a sweetened milky syrup.

RADHA   The milkmaid in Brindaban who was Krishna's beloved, though she was not his wife. To Vaishnavs in Bengal, Radha is the ultimate symbol of selfless love.

RAITA   Among Bengali Muslims, a salad of yoghurt and cucumbers.

RAJBHOG   A large spherical sweet made with *chhana*, floating in syrup. Similar to the *rasogolla*.

RAMZAN   Also called Ramadan, this is the holy month of fasting in the Islamic calendar, preceding the festival of Id-ul-fitr.

RAS   Literally, juice. Specifically it also means the first tapping of syrup from the trunk of the date-palm tree. Instead of being made into *gur*, this thin liquid is often drunk as a refreshing morning drink.

RASOGOLLAS   Perhaps the most famous Bengali sweet, along with *sandesh*. These are balls made with *chhana* and boiled in a plain syrup.

RASOMALAI   A kind of sweet with *rasogollas* floating in sweetened evaporated milk.

RATHAJATRA   The chariot festival, the major event for the Hindus during the monsoon month of Asharh.

RUI   The most prized variety of freshwater carp.

SANDESH   Like the *rasogolla*, a famous Bengali sweet made with *chhana*. It is sweetened with sugar or *gur* in the cooking, instead of being boiled in syrup.

SANKRANTI   The last day of any month.

SARASWATI PUJA   The worship of the goddess Saraswati, goddess of learning and music, during the spring.

SHAB-E-BARAT   Literally, the night of destiny. An important Muslim festival.

SHADH   Literally, wish or desire. It is also the term used for a special elaborate meal served to a pregnant woman towards the end of her pregnancy in the belief that if all her cravings are satisfied she will bear a healthy child.

SHAK   Any kind of leafy green, eaten as a vegetable.

SHAKTO   A Hindu sect, followers of Shakti, the mother goddess.

SHAPLA   The water lily, whose stems are eaten as a vegetable.

SHARAT   Early autumn.

SHASHTHI   The sixth day of the moon.

SHEET   Winter.

SHEETAL   Cool.

SHIDHDHA   Boiled. Parboiled rice is called *shidhdha chal*.

SHIM   A kind of buttery-textured flat bean, available in winter.

SHINGARA   Triangular flour shells stuffed with vegetables or meat and deep-fried in oil. A favourite with afternoon tea. These are better known outside Bengal as *samosas*.

SHOJNE/SHAJINA   A kind of long, stick-like pod, available during the spring and early summer, much prized as a delicacy and used in fish stews or mixed vegetable dishes.

SHOL   A kind of fish, mostly available in the winter and never eaten unless bought live.

SHORSHE   Mustard. Hilsa cooked in a mustard sauce is called *shorshe ilish*.

SHRADHDHA   The Hindu funeral ceremony.

SHUKTO   A bitter vegetable dish, served as a first course with rice, especially during the summer. *Shukto* is never served at dinner, only at lunch.

SINDUR   A vermilion powder worn by Hindu married women on their partings. Also an auspicious element, used to decorate the foreheads of goddesses.

TAAL   The fruit of the palm tree. *Taaler bara* means the small balls made by combining the pulp of the ripe fruit with coconut, flour and sugar and deep-frying them. A monsoon delight.

TATTO   The ceremonial array of gifts sent by the groom to his bride before the wedding. A West Bengali Hindu practice.

TELEBHAJA   Literally, fried in oil. A collective term denoting any of several vegetables dipped in batter and fried in oil as a savoury snack or to be served with rice.

TULSI   The wild basil which Bengali Vaishnavs consider holy since Krishna is supposed to have loved it.

UCHCHE   The smaller variety of bitter gourd.

VAISHNAV   Followers of Vishnu, one of whose incarnations was Krishna.

COMMON WAYS OF COOKING BENGALI FOOD

AMBAL   A sour dish made either with several vegetables or with fish, the sourness being produced by the addition of tamarind pulp or sour berries like *karamcha* or fruits like tomatoes or green mangoes. *Ambals* are meant to be eaten at the end of a meal, before dessert, and are more common in summer.

BHAJA   Anything fried, either by itself or in batter.

BHARTA or BHATE   Any vegetable, such as potatoes, beans, aubergines, pumpkins or even *dal*, first boiled whole, then mashed and seasoned with mustard oil and spices. Sometimes ghee is used instead of mustard oil. This is usually eaten as a first item with rice.

BHUNA   A Muslim term, meaning fried for a long time with ground and whole spices over high heat. Usually applied to meat.

CHACHCHARI   Usually a vegetable dish of one or more varieties of vegetables cut into longish strips, sometimes with the stalk of leafy greens added, all lightly seasoned with ground spices like mustard or poppy seeds and flavoured with a *phoron*. Small fish can be made into a *chachchari*, as can the skin and bones of large fish like bhetki or chitol. The latter is also called *kanta-chachchari, kanta* meaning bone.

CHHANCHRA   A combination dish made with different vegetables, portions of fish head and fish oil.

CHHENCHKI   Tiny pieces of one or more vegetable – or, sometimes even the peel (of potatoes, white gourd, pumpkin, cucumber or *patol*, for example) – usually flavoured with *panch phoron* or whole mustard seeds or *kalo jeera*. Chopped onion and garlic can also be used, but hardly any ground spices.

DALNA   Mixed vegetables or eggs, cooked in a medium-thick gravy seasoned with ground spices, especially *garom mashla* and a touch of ghee.

DAM   Vegetables, especially potatoes, or meat cooked in a covered pot slowly over a low heat.

GHANTO   A great stand-by dish, especially when guests come unexpectedly. Different complementary vegetables (e.g., cabbage, green peas, potatoes or banana blossom, coconut, chick-peas) are chopped or grated fine and cooked with both a *phoron* and with complex ground spices. Dried pellets of *dal* (*boris*) are often added to a *ghanto*. Ghee is commonly added at the end. In nineteenth-century East Bengal the *ghanto* was often called *beshwari*, probably from the medieval *beshoar* meaning dried and powdered. Non-vegetarian *ghantos* are also made, with fish or fish heads added to vegetables. The famous *murighanto* is made with fish heads cooked with a fine variety of rice. But fish *ghanto* is more common among the Hindus of East Bengal than in West Bengal. Some *ghantos* are very dry, others thick and juicy.

JHAL   Literally, hot. A great favourite in West Bengali households, this is made with fish or shrimp or crab, first lightly fried and then cooked in a light sauce of ground red chilli or ground mustard and a flavouring of *panch phoron* or *kalo jeera*. Being dryish, it is often eaten with a little bit of *dal* poured over the rice. In Bangladesh the term *jhal gosht* means a very hot and spicy preparation of beef or *khashi* meat, but it can also have a gravy.

JHOL   A light fish or vegetable stew seasoned with ground spices like ginger, cumin, coriander, chilli and turmeric, with pieces of fish and longitudinal slices of vegetables floating in it. The gravy is thin yet extremely flavourful, and is meant to be eaten with a lot of rice. Whole green chillies are usually added at the end and green coriander is used in season for extra taste.

KALIA   A very rich preparation of fish, meat or vegetables using a lot of oil and ghee with a sauce usually based on ground ginger and onion paste and *garom mashla*. Served at weddings and other festive occasions.

KORMA   A Muslim term, meaning meat or chicken cooked in a mild yoghurt-based sauce with ghee instead of oil. Some people use thick evaporated milk instead of yoghurt.

PORA   Literally, burnt. Though we do not have a closed oven for baking, many vegetables are wrapped in leaves and roasted over a wood or charcoal fire. Some, like aubergines, are put directly over the flames. Before eating, the roasted vegetable is mixed with oil and spices like a *bharta*.

TARKARI   A general term often used in Bengal the way 'curry' is used in English. Originally from Persian, the word first meant uncooked garden vegetables. From this it was a natural extension to mean cooked vegetables or even fish and vegetables cooked togther.

SUGGESTED MENUS

Boiled rice
Fried aubergine slices (p. 77)
Kancha moong dal (p. 43)
Lau-ghanto (p. 49)
Machher jhol (p. 46)
Sweet yoghurt

◊

Boiled rice
Shukto (p. 40)
Masoor dal (p. 44)
Lau-chingri (p. 48)
Fish in yoghurt sauce (p. 68)
Posto chutney (p. 63)

◊

Boiled rice
Alu posto (p. 64)
Patol in yoghurt sauce (p. 51)
Narkel chingri (p. 163)
Lamb with posto (p. 66)
Cucumber in yoghurt salad

◊

Plain polao (p. 159)
Roasted moong dal (p. 43)
Galda chingrir malaikari (p. 162)
Khashir rezala (p. 58)
Cucumber and tomato salad with
chopped coriander leaves

◊

Boiled rice
Masoor dal (p. 44)
Mochar ghanto (p. 89)
Fried hilsa pieces with hilsa oil (p. 92)
Hilsa with mustard (p. 93)

◊

Khichuri (pp. 74 and 76)
Fried aubergine slices (p. 77)
Fried pumpkin slices (p. 80)
Fried hilsa pieces with hilsa oil (p. 92)
Pineapple chutney (p. 102)

◊

Boiled rice
Lemon dal (p. 44)
Spring onions with shrimps and coconut (p. 85)
Pumpkin with coconut (p. 87)
Hilsa with coconut milk (p. 95)

◊

Boiled rice
Kalo jeera bharta (p. 103)
Kancha moong dal (p. 43)
Carp roe boras (p. 97)
Crab jhal (p. 98)

Luchis (p. 109)
Alur dam (p. 110)
Cabbage ghanto (p. 145)
Chholar dal (p. 111)
Chicken with posto (p. 65)
Payesh (p. 121)

◊

Plain polao (p. 159)
Cauliflower bhaji (p. 141)
Spiced roast aubergine (p. 131)
Roasted moong dal (p. 43)
Meat without onions and garlic (p. 114)
Sweet yoghurt and sweets

◊

Boiled rice
Gotasheddho (p. 144)
Potatoes cooked with green peas
and tomatoes (p. 140)
Masoor dal (p. 44)
Handi kabab (p. 159)

◊

Luchis (p. 109)
Dhonkar dalna (p. 134)
Duck bhuna (p. 156) *or*
Duck with coconut milk (p. 157)
Aubergine with tamarind (p. 146)
Orange-flavoured sweet rice (p. 171)

Index

TRADITIONAL MOROCCAN COOKING: RECIPES FROM FEZ

Madame Z. Guinaudeau

Foreword by Claudia Roden

Moroccan cuisine is famous for its subtle blending of spices, herbs and honey with meat and vegetables. In Fez, the country's culinary centre, the cooking has numerous influences – Arab and Berber, with hints of Jewish, African and French. The country's classic dishes are the famous *couscous, tagines* or stews, and *bistilla*, an exquisite pie made with flaky pastry.

Capturing the atmosphere of Fez, cultural capital of the medieval Moorish world, Madame Guinaudeau takes us behind closed doors into the kitchens and dining rooms of the old city. She invites us to a banquet in a wealthy home, shopping in the spice market and to the potter's workshop; shares with us the secrets of preserving lemons for a *tagine*; shows us how to make Moroccan bread.

Traditional Moroccan Cooking is the perfect introduction to a splendid culinary heritage and a vivid description of an ancient and beautiful city. It offers a taste of the delights to be found in one of the world's great gastronomic centres.

'Successfully evokes the magical flavours of Fez.'
Nigel Slater, *Observer*

'Wonderful descriptions of the food
and how to cook it.'
Thane Prince, *Daily Telegraph*

paperback

also published by Serif

CLASSIC JAMAICAN COOKING: TRADITIONAL RECIPES AND HERBAL REMEDIES

Caroline Sullivan

Foreword by Cristine MacKie

Okra, plantains, sweet potatoes and mangoes: these and the other essential ingredients of Jamaican cooking are now widely available in Britain and America, bringing the island's delicious cooking within anyone's reach.

Covering all aspects of Jamaican cuisine from soups to preserves, fish to ices, *Classic Jamaican Cooking* also presents a range of traditional herbal remedies and drinks. With recipes as varied as plantain tart and okra soup, salt fish patties and coconut ice-cream, this book dispels forever the myth that Jamaican cookery begins with curried goat and ends with rice and peas.

Needing only occasional modification for the modern reader ('Take seven gallons of rum, three gallons of seville orange-juice …'), Caroline Sullivan brings alive the wealth and variety of the island's food.

'A wealth of very good recipes.'
Frances Bissell, *Times*

'Wonderful ideas that will appeal to adventurous cooks.'
Lindsey Bareham

paperback

COOKING IN TEN MINUTES

Edouard de Pomiane

Foreword by Raymond Blanc

300 uncomplicated *and* delicious recipes by France's most creative cookery writer, the witty, irreverent and super-efficient Edouard de Pomiane. Whizzing from stove to table, and still keeping everything under control, he delights us with his joy in cooking and with his belief that good food need not be the sole preserve of people with vast amounts of time and money to spend. This book is a must for anyone who leads a busy life but is determined to create the space in which to eat well.

'The very best kind of cookery writing.'
Elizabeth David

'An utter delight.'
Philippa Davenport, *Financial Times*

'Both timeless and timely, Pomiane's stylish good sense never dates.'
Geraldene Holt

'An inspirational energy and joy in cooking.'
Guardian

paperback

COOKING WITH POMIANE

Edouard de Pomiane

Foreword by Elizabeth David

Dashing, mocking, conspiratorial, *Cooking With Pomiane* gives the best advice you could ever hope for on the making of meals both simple and spectacular. Writing in clear, logical language, Pomiane describes how to prepare each recipe with wit, ease and fluency. Like a good friend, he understands the difficulties of real cooking and shopping; he sympathises, makes a joke of our blunders, brushes them aside and breezes on. Throughout, he refuses to show off with his specialist's expertise and explains things with great common sense in the most engaging way, infecting us with his sheer love of food and zest for good cooking.

'Both serious and funny, never pompous, and enjoyably anti-slimming.'
Michèle Roberts, *Sunday Times*

'Besides being practical – de Pomiane really makes you understand what goes on when you boil, fry, roast, grill and braise – these books are enormous fun to read.'
Paul Levy, *Daily Mail*

'You will love him and his writing.'
Spectator

paperback

also published by Serif

THE ALICE B. TOKLAS COOKBOOK

Foreword by Maureen Duffy

The Alice B. Toklas Cookbook is one of the few books which truly deserve the label 'legendary'. Toklas lived with Gertrude Stein, the American writer and art collector, in Paris and the Bugey, a rural area in south-eastern France famous for its cooking. For more than 25 years she collected and adapted recipes with which she entertained Picasso, Matisse and others. The fruit of hundreds of hours in the kitchen, market-place and vegetable-garden, this entertaining culinary companion ranges from inventive responses to wartime austerity to full-blown French bourgeois cooking at its richest and best. Always delicious, the recipes here vary from simple snacks – mushroom sandwiches and tricolour omelette made with spinach and tomato – to more complex dishes like *suprême of pike à la Dijonaise* and pheasant with cottage cheese.

The Alice B. Toklas Cookbook has long enjoyed a reputation as one of the most original cookbooks of the twentieth century. Available once again, it is certain to delight a new generation of readers as well as find its way back onto shelves from where it has mysteriously disappeared.

'A delightful concoction of reminiscences and recipes.'
Time Out

paperback

HOME BAKED:
A LITTLE BOOK OF
BREAD RECIPES

George and Cecilia Scurfield

Foreword by Paul Bailey

Home baking has once again become one of the most popular forms of cookery, and this highly praised book is the perfect introduction to the subject for anyone who has wanted to make their own bread but feared that baking is too complicated or time-consuming. *Home Baked* starts with a clear summary of how to go about quickly acquiring the skills of kneading, rising, proving and baking itself. As in all forms of cookery, a bread's appearance is almost as important as its flavour, and the Scurfields describe how to transform a tasty but ordinary-looking bread into something supremely attractive and appetising.

Home Baked is essential kitchen equipment for those who suspect that bread-making can be more rewarding than warming up a deep-frozen 'French stick' from a supermarket but thought that they could never get the dough to rise.

'That lovable little volume on yeast cookery.'
Elizabeth David

'An inspiring, comprehensive and apparently fool-proof little book.'
Times Literary Supplement

paperback

HOME-MADE CAKES AND BISCUITS

George and Cecilia Scurfield

Foreword by Geraldene Holt

What could be more useful than a short, unpretentious introduction to the art of cake-making? Starting with simple recipes, the reader is gradually introduced to a full range of cakes including those made with nuts, chocolate and fruit both fresh and dried. Unlike over-sweet cakes bought from shops, those made at home can be completely free of additives and colouring – and twice as tasty.

Home-Made Cakes and Biscuits contains recipes for cakes that will appeal to children as well as adults, cakes for special occasions and for every day. There are also clear, concise and practical recipes for pastries, biscuits, icing and fillings. The recipes come from England, America, France and Austria. With easy-to-follow recipes for such delights as Rich Chocolate Cake, Viennese Orange Cake, Nusstorte, Hazel Nut Macaroons and French Plum Cake, tea-time need never again be reduced to a packet of biscuits fast approaching its sell-by date.

'Delightful.'
A La Carte

'As welcome as the return of the swallows.'
Elisabeth Luard, *Scotsman*

paperback